The Fair M
of Guildford

and other Surrey tales

The Fair Maid of Guildford

and other Surrey tales

Matthew Alexander

with Illustrations by Don Osmond

COUNTRYSIDE BOOKS

NEWBURY · BERKSHIRE

COUNTRYSIDE BOOKS
3 CATHERINE ROAD
NEWBURY, BERKSHIRE

To view our complete range of books,
please visit us at
www.countrysidebooks.co.uk

ISBN 1 85306 827 6

To my wife Mary

Cover designed by Peter Davies, Nautilus Design
Produced through MRM Associates Ltd., Reading
Printed in England by J.W. Arrowsmith Ltd., Bristol

Contents

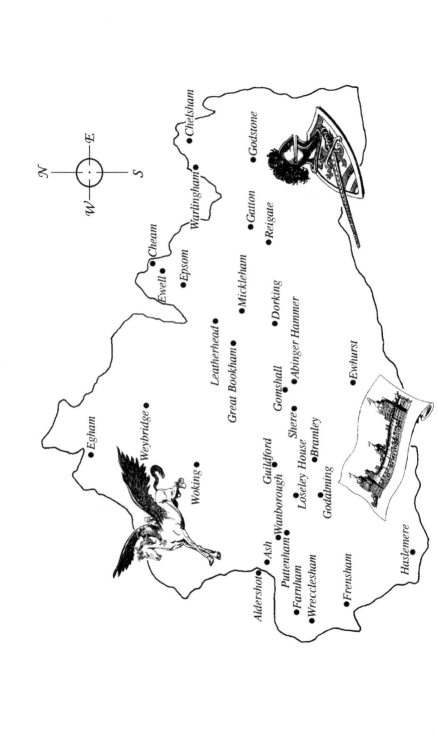

CONTENTS

The Fair Maid of Guildford

IN 1485 SIR THOMAS MALORY published a remarkable book. *Le Morte d'Arthur* was a collection of tales of King Arthur and the Knights of the Round Table gathered from a number of sources. It included one particularly poignant tale of unrequited love which links Guildford with Arthurian legend.

The story tells how King Arthur decreed, at his court at Westminster, a grand tournament to be held at 'Camelot' (which Malory thought was Winchester). The court duly set off, leaving behind only Queen Guinevere and Sir Lancelot, who made the excuse that they were ill. In fact they were having a love affair. Guinevere, however, warned Lancelot against arousing suspicion and urged him to follow the others. The next day he rode out towards Winchester and stopped for the night 'in a town called Astolat, that is now in English called Guildford'. An old knight, Sir Bernard, welcomed him to his house near the castle. Lancelot decided to attend the tournament in disguise, and asked Sir Bernard for a shield, as the arms painted on his own were too well known. Sir Bernard willingly agreed that he should have the shield of his elder son who was recovering from a wound, and that his younger son, Sir Lavaine, should ride with him to the tournament.

9

While these arrangements were being made, the host's daughter gazed longingly at the handsome stranger. For the beautiful Elaine, known as 'The Fair Maid of Astolat', had fallen in love at first sight. She begged Sir Lancelot to wear her token at the joust. Lancelot, who was famous for never wearing a token or favour, was just about to refuse when he remembered that he was going in disguise. Accordingly he accepted one of her scarlet, pearl-embroidered sleeves, not for her sake, but to allay any suspicion that he might be Lancelot.

As the day of the joust drew near Sir Lancelot left his own shield in Elaine's safe-keeping and set out for Winchester with Sir Lavaine. In a field outside the town a stand had been set up for spectators, from which King Arthur watched the two sides fight. The Knights of the Round Table fought the visiting challengers.

Lancelot and Lavaine watched from the edge of a wood as Arthur's knights drove back the strangers – and then charged into the fray against the Round Tablers. Both fought well, but none fought better than Sir Lancelot until he was wounded in the side by a spear-thrust from his old friend, Sir Bors, who naturally had not recognised him. A fanfare heralded the end of the contest, and the unknown knight wearing the favour of a scarlet sleeve was declared the winner. But he was nowhere to be found. Still wishing to remain incognito, Lancelot had painfully ridden away with Lavaine to a hermitage nearby where an old surgeon tended his wound.

A day or two after the end of the tournament, King Arthur's court set out to return to London. Sir Gawain, a close friend of Sir Lancelot, happened by chance to seek lodgings at Sir Bernard's house in Guildford. He told his host, and his attentive daughter, of the courage and skill of the unknown knight who had worn the scarlet sleeve. Elaine rejoiced to hear of her beloved's prowess and triumphantly produced the shield she had lovingly kept. Gawain immediately recognised it as Lancelot's and, knowing that he must be badly wounded, declared his intention of finding him. Elaine, concerned for Lancelot's health, insisted on going with him.

As they searched the area near Winchester, the pair met with Sir Lavaine, who guided them to the hermitage, where Elaine nursed Lancelot gradually back to health.

Several months passed before Lancelot was fit and well again. Fit and well enough, in fact, to distinguish himself at the next joust at Winchester. Afterwards he escorted Elaine back to her father's house in Guildford, and was about to leave her there when she burst into tears and begged him to marry her. When he refused she was desperate enough to implore him to take her as his mistress, feeling that she could not live without him. The chivalrous knight, however, would not stoop so low and offered her instead a thousand pounds a year to marry some other knight. At this, Elaine fainted and was carried to her room. Sir Lancelot felt very sorry for her but protested that he had given her no encouragement. He then left for the court at Westminster.

For ten days the broken hearted Elaine wept, neither sleeping nor eating. After such a rejection she felt life held nothing further for her and determined to die. She called her father and brother and asked for a letter to be written, which she clasped in her right hand. She then gave instructions for her body to be laid in a richly decorated bed, taken to the Thames and floated down the river to Westminster. This was duly done.

At Westminster Lancelot, idly looking out of a palace window, saw a black-draped barge coming, bearing a golden bed on which lay the body of a beautiful woman 'who lay as though she had smiled'. The note gripped in her lifeless hand was addressed to him. It asked him to pay for her funeral. This he did, with all the court and the Knights of the Round Table in attendance. Sir Lancelot regretted her death, but as he said 'Love must arise of the heart and not by no constraint.'

11

The Wey Navigation

THE RIVER WEY rises in Hampshire and flows eastwards and then northwards through the gap is has cut in the Downs at Guildford to join the Thames at Weybridge. Just to the north of Guildford it loops round the estate of Sutton Place, home in the early 17th century of Sir Richard Weston. He was a forward-thinking man, interested in improving agriculture, and as part of his experiments in irrigation and drainage in 1620 he completed his 'Flowing River', a short artificial canal with a lock.

He realised that to canalise the whole length of the river from the Thames to Guildford would not only be a practical proposition but would also bring great commercial benefit to the town, which at that time was suffering a depression following the collapse of the wool trade. The next year saw a petition from the Mayor of Guildford for an Act of Parliament to make this possible, but this failed to be passed in 1624. Other unsuccessful attempts followed and it was not until after the Civil Wars in 1651 that the necessary Act was passed, empowering the Corporation to dig through riverside owners' lands and other works. Weston himself, though, was politically suspect, being a Roman Catholic and a Royalist sympathiser.

It was a Roundhead soldier, Major James Pitson, who took over as a leading figure in the undertaking, together with Richard Scotcher. Work began in August 1651, but Weston died the following year before seeing his scheme completed. It involved cutting nine miles of canal and building twelve locks, and by the time it was opened in November 1653 the actual cost had wildly exceeded the estimate of £6,000. Over £15,000 was spent, in fact, and from the first the Wey Navigation was hampered by debts and squabbles among the shareholders. Pitson was suspected of embezzlement and amid the tangle and confusion of the finances, Scotcher felt he had been hard done by.

However muddled the accounts, there was no doubt that the Navigation was a great success. It was not the first such river navigation in the country but it was an extensive one and made use of the 'pound' locks developed on the Continent. Barges were able to travel from the London docks up to the wharf just downstream of Guildford Bridge, and the town profited greatly from the increased trade that this brought. On the other hand, finances were made even more complicated in 1660, when the original Cromwellian Act was declared invalid at the Restoration. A new Act of Parliament was passed in 1671, which tried to straighten out the confused finances of the Navigation by appointing trustees who paid dividends to the shareholders and tolls to the Guildford Corporation and two riverside land-owners. There were still disputes about ownership of shares, however, and it was not until the 18th century that the shares came into the hands of two proprietors only, the Langtons of Lincolnshire and the Earls of Portmore of Weybridge.

The principal goods carried on the Navigation were corn (especially wheat) and timber, including wooden hoops for barrels. Gunpowder from the mills at Chilworth was an important cargo until after the First World War, and increasingly coal and imported timber came upstream, together with a multiplicity of other goods. It is possible that passengers were also carried for a time, in a 'Fly' boat.

The success of the Wey Navigation prompted the making of the Godalming Navigation, which extended the navigable river up to Godalming and was completed in 1764. Other waterways followed: the Basingstoke Canal of 1794, and the Wey and Arun Junction Canal of 1816. Both used the Wey Navigation as part of their route to London, but neither flourished and, following the coming of the railways, both failed in mid-Victorian times. The Wey Navigation itself survived the railway challenge, on the other hand, carrying bulk goods commercially right up until 1969 – and there was even a brief revival of grain transport to Coxes Lock Mill in the 1980s.

The ownership of the Navigation passed through several hands in the last century until in 1902 it came into the possession of the Stevens family, who had been the managers for three generations. They later acquired the Godalming Navigation also, although they continued to be run as two separate concerns. The massive Wey barges themselves were built at Dapdune Wharf until the Second World War. They were 70 to 80 feet long and over 14 feet wide, being capable of carrying loads of 80 to 90 tons. Man-hauling, and later horse-drawing, was the rule, but some barges had spritsails for use in a favourable wind – and of course rowing and poling was required for some manoeuvres. With the coming of steam power, tugs would haul the barges up from the docks to Weybridge. As the journey rarely lasted more than a day, it was unnecessary to provide full living accommodation on board, although some barges had a small cabin in the stern for use, say, when a barge had to wait at the docks for several days for a full cargo. Perhaps because the Wey barges were rarely lived in for any length of time, they never developed the elaborate painted decoration associated with the narrowboats of the North and Midlands.

By the 1960s it was clear that cargo-carrying on the Wey was becoming uneconomic, and in 1963 Mr. Harry Stevens gave the Wey Navigation to the National Trust, followed by the gift of the Godalming Navigation in 1968. Two years later the Guildford Wharf and the Navigation offices in Friary Street were demolished to make way for a new embankment and shops. Not everything was destroyed, however. The great treadwheel crane which had loaded and unloaded the barges was carefully dismantled and rebuilt near its original site on the new embankment. The 18 foot wheel inside the crane-house was operated by men walking backwards and forwards inside it. Now only pleasure craft chug past it, but it stands as a mute reminder of one of the earliest and most successful river navigations in England.

Epsom Spa
and
the Derby

T HE SURREY TOWN of Epsom is known today throughout
the world. In the early 17th century it was merely a
village like many another along the North Downs but it
rose to prominence because of two principal factors: the
eponymous Epsom Salts and the annual horse-race known
as the Derby.

The story begins in the dry summer of 1618, when a
certain Henry Whicker noticed that thirsty cattle refused
to drink from a spring on Epsom Common. He found that
it had a distinctly unpleasant taste, and accordingly realised that the water might have medicinal properties (it
being well known, then as now, that anything that tastes
nasty must do you good). In fact the water contained
magnesium sulphate, soon to become famous as Epsom
Salts, and its aperient qualities were recognised and valued.
A wall was built round the spring, and a shed to provide
shelter for the invalids who began to visit in increasing
numbers in the hope of improving their health. By the
time of the Restoration in 1660, the spa at Epsom had
acquired a reputation among London society. Charles II
himself came to take the waters, as did many of his courtiers and hangers-on, and not forgetting Nell Gwynne.

The ubiquitous Samuel Pepys visited on at least two occasions, noting with surprise how many Londoners could afford to travel to Epsom. Certainly the town was closer to the metropolis than Tunbridge Wells, its only rival spa, and soon Epsom was providing the entertainments demanded by the throng of wealthy visitors, who had come to purge themselves of the effects of similar self-indulgence in London. In 1690 an area of the common 450 yards in diameter was enclosed around the well, with buildings and tree-lined avenues for the comfort of the visitors. Splendid assembly rooms were built in the High Street, and Epsom Spa reached the peak of its popularity at the end of the 17th century – indeed, the principal attractions came to be the dances, the horse-races, and other entertainments rather than the unpalatable laxative water itself.

In 1706 a quack doctor named Levingstone decided to cash in on Epsom's success. He built another Assembly Room in the High Street and sunk his New Well in a spot conveniently near the town. When in 1715 he acquired the lease of the original well, he closed it down, hoping to transfer the business to his New Well. Unfortunately, the water from the New Well tasted quite different from that of the Old Well – it was quite pleasant, in fact, and therefore quite worthless. The popularity of Epsom as a health resort declined rapidly and although the Old Well was reopened in 1727, sea-bathing had become the fashionable health-cure of the day and Epsom never regained its former glory.

Horse-racing, though, continued as a gentleman's sport on the chalk downs south of the town. The short grass and the undulating ground made them an ideal test for the stamina of young horses – four-mile races from Banstead to Epsom Downs were regular events. In 1769 Dennis O'Kelly's *Eclipse* won with an astonishing lead. '*Eclipse* first, the rest nowhere', as he said in a phrase that was to become famous. Subsequently, long odds on made it pointless to continue racing him, but *Eclipse* went on to sire many successful racehorses. It can be said, indeed, that most horses running today can claim some trace of his blood in their ancestry. *Eclipse* was born too soon, however, to run in the Derby.

In 1779 the Earl of Derby held a house-party at The Oaks, Woodmansterne. The drunken revellers decided that a new kind of horse-race was needed, without the exhausting preliminary heats that were then customary. Accordingly this race was run at Epsom, for three-year-old fillies and colts, and was named after the house where the carousing sportsmen had met. The Oaks was an immediate success, and the following year another race was inaugurated, solely for fillies. Tradition has it that the Earl of Derby tossed a coin with the leading sportsman Sir Charles Bunbury to decide after which of them the race should be named. Like so many tales of old Surrey, regrettably, there is no evidence to support this. Nevertheless, if true, then Sir Charles had his revenge when his horse *Diomed* won the first Derby on 4th May 1780.

The Derby, with its shorter distance and higher stakes, was more exciting than other races and Epsom once more began to see the fashionable – and not so fashionable – flocking into the town in the week before Whitsun. By Victorian times, Derby Day had become a great national festival. Rich and poor mingled as equals amid the bookmakers, the gypsies, and the pickpockets – even the House of Commons suspended business on Derby Day and during the Crimean War the result was included in the official orders dispatched from England. Stands – nay, grand stands – were built for the refined spectators, while the less refined gathered on the Hill opposite, a colourful swirl of humanity from all over London and the countryside around.

There is little in Epsom today which preserves the memory of the spa. The original Assembly Rooms of 1690 are now home to Wetherspoons pub, and the Old Well itself is forlornly isolated behind railings in the centre of a modern housing estate that fills its once-spacious circular enclosure. The Derby, however, is alive and well, and still retains its magic. Many people, throughout the world, become gamblers once a year on Derby Day, and the crowds throng the historic turf of Epsom Downs.

The Pharisees

THE PEOPLE of old Surrey believed in the little people. These the country people called the 'fairieses', with the dialect 'double plural'. This came to be associated with the Biblical 'Pharisees' and thus it was always written. The pharisees were not the tiny gossamer-winged fairies of Victorian children's books, but people, smaller than humans but of their form and with all their faults and virtues. They were, however, supernatural beings, coming from another world different both from Heaven and Hell. They were believed to live separate but similar lives from the human world, but could intervene in mortal affairs if they so wished. Sometimes they were benevolent, sometimes mischievous, but usually they simply indulged their own whims and caprices.

The most commonly reported – and most irritating – of the pharisees' habits apparently was riding horses at night. The carter would come down to unlock the stable early in the morning to prepare them for the day's work, only to find them sweating and panting in their stalls. Of course, the less wise might suggest they had caught a fever, but it was clear to the horseman that the pharisees had been riding them all night, leaving them exhausted. Each pharisee had his favourite mount, he knew, and would ride no other, tying knots in the horse's mane to act as stirrups as he rode astride its neck. Any tangles found in the hair of the mane would confirm this. Some accounts differ, though, and blame the night-riding on witches, or on the terrifying Night Hag, a sinister being which not only torments horses but also the carter himself. As he sleeps, the Night Hag mounts upon his chest, crushing him into the bed. The only way to prevent these visitations is to sleep with a Bible under the pillow.

There are several courses of action which can be adopted, however, to prevent horses being hag-ridden. One is to suspend a flint with a natural hole through it over the horse's stall. Another is to nail a sickle or scythe blade to the manger. Perhaps the most popular was the nailing of a horseshoe around the keyhole: it was known that the pharisees flew in through keyholes but had an antipathy for iron. This practice still has its echoes in the present day in the nailing of horseshoes over stable doors 'for luck'.

On the other hand, the pharisees could do humans a good turn if they felt so minded. They would help with the harvest, or mowing the sweet grass in the meadows at haymaking time. This would always be done in the dark of the night, when no mortals were about to see them at work. Indeed, it was considered bad luck to spy on the pharisees – as is borne out by a tale told by Harry Hart of Puttenham to the curate, Francis Kerry, in 1869.

'A farm servant was employed to thresh wheat in his master's barn, but every morning to his great surprise he found that a considerable quantity had been knocked out during the night. His curiosity was roused, so he resolved to discover, if possible, his mysterious assistants. Having seated himself one night on a beam in the mow, after a while he saw two diminutive beings enter the barn and seize each of them a flail. To work they went for a considerable time: at length one of them, pausing, said to the other, 'I sweat; do you?' upon which the man shouted from his beam 'And the d...l sweat both of you!' They vanished instantly, and from that very night the fairies never again visited the barn.'

By all accounts the farm labourer got off lightly: others who were discovered spying on the pharisees suffered bad luck or even death.

The pharisees were very particular about the state of the hearth in the farmhouses. When all had gone to bed, they would fly in through the keyhole and disport themselves around the warm ashes of the fire. A tidy housemaid would have swept the hearth carefully and left a basin of water for the 'Good People'. In the morning the basin would be empty and a silver coin would be lying in it as a reward. If they found the hearth unswept and neglected, on the other hand, the pharisees would fly upstairs and pinch the servants black and blue as they slept as a punishment for their laziness. Indeed, it is not uncommon for people to find small, inexplicable bruises on themselves without being aware of any injury that might have caused them. Perhaps, just perhaps, the pharisees are still in the habit of night-visiting, and of making their own trenchant comments on bad housework in their own individual way.

Fanny Burney

Frances Burney, or Madame d'Arblay as she became, had a particular affection for the county of Surrey, especially for the Mole valley between Leatherhead and Dorking. For it was here that she found friendship, happiness and love.

The daughter of a musician, Fanny Burney spent much of her childhood writing secret stories. One tale in particular developed in her mind until she finally wrote it down and published it as a novel in 1778, under the title of *Evelina*. It was an immediate success. The 26 year-old authoress was staying at Chessington Hall, the home of a dear family friend, Samuel Crisp, when she heard that the great Dr Johnson had praised her book. She was so transported with pleasure at the approval of such a famous literary critic that she danced a jig around a mulberry tree in the garden. She was to meet Samuel Johnson himself at the home of the celebrated Mrs Thrale at Streatham not far away, and the two literary ladies became friends. Fanny's second novel, *Cecilia*, was completed in 1782 and was similarly received with adulation. She spent many days at the home of the Locks, old family friends, at Norbury Park near Mickleham, drinking in 'that contentment which Norbury Park seems to have gathered from all corners of the world'.

In 1786 Fanny accepted a position as maid to Queen Charlotte, but was not happy at court. Her position was more menial than honourable, although the Queen liked her writings and appreciated her sympathy when George III fell into one of his fits of madness. When she left court life in 1791, Fanny toured England before coming to stay once more at Mickleham, where her married sister was living. It was to prove a turning point in her life.

At Juniper Hall nearby there lived a group of French emigrés, monarchists who had fled from the terrors of the Revolution. They included the devious politician Talleyrand and the intellectual Madame de Staël. Among them also was General Alexandre d'Arblay, tall, intelligent, and amusing. When they met in January 1793 Fanny fell in love with him, and he with her. 'He has a sincerity, a frankness, an ingenuous openness of nature' she wrote, 'that I had been unjust enough to think could not belong to a Frenchman.' Indeed, England was then at war with Revolutionary France and anti-French feeling ran high, even against those Frenchmen opposed to the Revolution. Nevertheless, after going to Chessington to think matters over, Fanny decided to accept his proposal of marriage.

Fanny Burney became Madame d'Arblay at Mickleham church in July 1793, and the ceremony was repeated a few days later in a Roman Catholic chapel to ensure that the marriage would be recognised if ever d'Arblay could return to France. Her father, while consenting, disapproved of the match and did not attend the wedding. His objection was not d'Arblay's nationality, but his poverty. There was only Fanny's royal pension of £100 yearly to support them. Both were determined to make a success of married life, however, and they rented a farmhouse at Fairfield, Great Bookham. Here their son Alexander was born in 1795, while Fanny was working on her next novel. In her letters she writes with affection and amusement of her military husband, trimming a hedge with mighty slashes of his sabre, or uprooting a whole bed of asparagus plants, thinking them to be weeds.

Their friends the Locks leased them a small plot of land on the Norbury Park estate at West Humble. It commanded a wonderful view of the Mole valley, and here the couple decided to build a permanent home. Money was short, but Fanny's third novel, *Camilla* was published in 1796, and brought in enough to pay for the building. The following year the d'Arblays moved into 'Camilla Cottage', as it was appropriately named, but their stay there was to be shorter than either had expected. The Peace of Amiens in 1801 enabled General d'Arblay to return to his native France. He had hopes of a military appointment, but these were unfulfilled because, in gratitude to the land which had sheltered him as a refugee, he insisted that he should never be asked to fight Englishmen. Despite this, Fanny joined her husband in France, and they were both there when Napoleon once again declared war on England. After the wars had ended in 1815, Fanny could once more return to England but in fact she spent little time in Surrey in the remaining years until her death in 1840.

Fanny d'Arblay's later books, it must be said, were never quite as good as her early novels. It is on these that her reputation largely rests, together with her letters and diaries. Her novels were influential, and Fanny Burney was one of the few contemporary authoresses whom Jane Austen esteemed highly. Some of the Surrey homes which resounded to Fanny Burney's laughter or intellectual conversation still stand today. Though Chessington Hall was rebuilt in 1803, Norbury Park is much as she knew it. Juniper Hall is now a Field Studies Centre, and Fairfield at Great Bookham has been renamed The Hermitage. Camilla Cottage, however, has changed out of all recognition. Extensively enlarged under the name Camilla Lacey, it is now submerged in a housing estate. In general, though, little has changed since the d'Arblays walked the Surrey Hills, at peace with the world, in those precious early years of marriage. 'Here we are tranquil, undisturbed and undisturbing. Can life ... be more innocent than ours or happiness more inoffensive'.

Mother Ludlam
and the
Frensham Cauldron

IN THE NORTH AISLE of Frensham church is an old copper cauldron, some thirty inches across and two feet deep, standing on an iron trivet. A little over three miles away, on a hillside overlooking the ruins of Waverley Abbey, is a cave from which flows a clear stream. Legend has woven a story that connects the cauldron and the cave – indeed, it is one of the oldest traditional tales of Surrey of which we have a record. It is particularly interesting to observe how details of the legend have changed over the years.

The first account is from John Aubrey, who heard the tale when he visited Frensham in 1673. 'In the Vestry here ... is an extraordinary great Kettle or Cauldron, which the Inhabitants say, by Tradition, was brought hither by the Fairies, Time out of Mind, from Borough Hill, about a mile hence. To this place, if any went to borrow a yoke of Oxen, Money, etc. he might have it for a Year or longer, so he kept his word to return it. On this Borough Hill ... is a great Stone lying along, of the Length of about six Feet. They went to this Stone, and knocked at it, and declared what they would borrow and when they would repay, and a Voice would answer when they should come and that they should find what they desir'd to borrow at that Stone. This Cauldron, with the Trivet, was borrow'd here after the Manner aforesaid, but not return'd according to

Promise; and though the Cauldron was afterwards carried to the Stone, it could not be received, and ever since that Time no Borrowing there.'

This account makes no mention of the cave at Moor Park, however. The first version that connects the cauldron with the cave is that heard by Frederick Grose, writing in 1785. He describes how the cave was laid out as a sort of grotto with stonework and seats by Sir William Temple of Moor Park earlier in that century. He calls it Mother Ludlam's Hole. 'This place derives its name from a popular story, which makes it formerly the residence of a white witch called Mother Ludlam, or Ludlow ... Mother Ludlam, instead of injuring, when properly invoked kindly assisted her poor neighbours in their necessities, by lending them such culinary utensils and household furniture as they wanted for particular occasions. The business was thus transacted: the petitioner went to the cave at midnight, turned three times round, and thrice repeated aloud, 'pray, good mother Ludlam, lend me such a thing (naming the utensil), and I will return it within two days'. He or she then retired and coming again early the next morning found at the entrance the requested moveable. This ... continued a long time till once a person not returning a large cauldron according to the stipulated time, madam Ludlam was so irritated at this want of punctuality that she refused to take it back when afterwards left in the cavern; and from that time to this has not accommodated anyone with the most trifling loan. The story adds that the cauldron was carried to Waverley Abbey, and after the dissolution of that monastery deposited in Frensham church.'

The outline of the story is certainly the same, but the location has been changed and this time it is a witch, not the fairies, who is the generous provider. In 1869, though, a very different version was told by the Rev. Beynham of Seale to Francis Kerry, Curate of Puttenham, who had also heard the earlier form of the tale. Kerry describes the cauldron or 'kettle' and then goes on: 'From an old tradition it would seem ... that the kettle has had at least one hair-breadth escape before it reached Frensham Church. It is said to have belonged originally to a witch who lived in a cave named ... "Mother Ludlam's Cave". To this place resorted all who had some ungratified desire which would surely be accomplished if the wisher only dropped a coin into this cauldron. One night, however, Satan stole the kettle and made off with it in the direction of the "Devil's Jumps": whether he carried his burden on his head, or under his arm, it is not certain, but the tripod must have accompanied it: ... Possibly, having lost his hold of the kettle, he may have thrown the tripod after it as of little use without the cauldron. Be this as it may, the vessel was found on "Kettlebury Hill" ... on which it is said to have fallen in its wonderful course when he leaped from one of these hills to the other.' The lending element is less emphasised in this variant, and another location, the Devil's Jumps, has been added – not to mention the Devil himself.

Yet another account comes from an old lady born in Wrecclesham in 1846 and who died in 1937. 'Mother Ludlam was a witch and a herbalist and the people came to her for help and potions, which she made in a large cauldron. One day Mr Nick came and asked her to lend him her cauldron. Mother Ludlam saw his foot marks in the sand, those of a goat, and refused. While her back was turned Mr Nick seized the cauldron and made off with it. Mother Ludlam mounted her broomstick and flew after him. The Devil had his seven league boots, and fleeing from Mother Ludlam, made seven great leaps. At each leap a hill arose, which are the Jumps. He left the cauldron on the last and highest called Kettlebury Hill and disappeared forming the Devil's Punchbowl in the side of Hindhead. Mother Ludlam picked up her cauldron and took it to Frensham Church for safety, where it can be seen to this day.'

So it may be seen that, far from being handed down unaltered over the years, local legends can change quite markedly and different versions can be current at the same time. Whatever the origins of these stories, though, Mother Ludlam's Cave still remains, though sadly neglected now, on the public footpath through Moor Park, and the cauldron may still be seen in Frensham church – almost certainly having been used in Tudor times to prepare food or drink for the parish 'ales' or feasts. Perhaps they are waiting for yet another yarn to be spun around them.

Wealden Iron

ARCHAEOLOGISTS chart the progress of mankind by the material used for tools, from the stone tools of earliest times to copper and bronze, and ultimately to iron. Iron was by far the most versatile and strongest material and, in the form of steel, is the most commonly used to this day. There is a long history of iron-making in England and the Weald of Surrey, Sussex, and Kent played an important, but largely forgotten part in this story.

The earliest ironworkings so far discovered in Surrey were at Dry Hill, Lingfield and Hascombe Camp, where iron was being produced before the Romans came. The Romans themselves developed the Wealden industry extensively, though mainly outside Surrey. The Middle Ages saw scattered ironworks in Surrey – at Thundersfield Castle, Alstead, and Charlwood, for example. All these early sites used the 'bloomery' process of manufacturing iron. The ore was obtained as nodules of clay ironstone from the Weald Clay, in early times by digging shallow pits but later by excavating deeper shafts. Often the spoil or waste from these shafts would be dumped in a previously worked-out shaft, leaving a shallow, circular depression when the fill settled. Many of these hollows can be seen in woodlands in the south west of the county. Minepit Copse between Wormley and Chiddingfold is an example of this.

The ore, or 'mine' as it was called, was then taken to the bloomery itself. This was in effect a simple kiln, constructed on a saucer-shaped base of clay onto which were piled alternate layers of charcoal and iron ore, and a clay covering put over the resulting heap to form a dome. The charcoal would then be ignited and bellows around the sides of the bloomery would raise the temperature high enough to smelt the iron. After a few hours of intense heat, the bloomery would be allowed to cool down and when it was dismantled a mass of iron – the 'bloom' – was found at the bottom beneath a layer of slag. There was cinder mixed in with the iron, and this had to be hammered out at a forge. This left 'wrought' or malleable iron, ready for the blacksmith to work.

These bloomeries were often quite small, needing only a few men – perhaps a family – to work them. As each was destroyed after firing, none actually survives: only the waste slag and cinder remain to show where they once had been. The names 'Cinderfield' at Horley and 'Cinderhill' at Godstone betray early ironworking sites.

The scale of ironmaking and the commercial basis on which it was undertaken changed dramatically at the end of the Middle Ages with the introduction into England of the blast furnace. This was a tower of stone or brick, loaded from the top with barrow-loads of charcoal and ore. They were much larger than the bloomeries and the huge bellows for the blasts of air they needed had to be powered by waterwheels. The higher temperatures obtained in this way produced molten iron, which could be run off from a tap-hole at the base of the furnace and poured directly into moulds. This 'cast' iron was harder and more brittle than the 'wrought' iron of the bloomery, and could not be used by a blacksmith until the cast-iron ingots or 'pigs' had been reheated and hammered with a large, water-driven trip-hammer in a forge. Repeated heating and hammering turned it into wrought iron.

This was a large-scale operation. Wealthy entrepreneurs

were needed to set up the specialised buildings and plant, and to employ large numbers of workers. Some furnaces had their own forges, such as those at Thursley, Vachery, and Burningfold near Dunsfold. Other furnaces sold their pig iron to independent forges, such as Abinger Hammer. The fuel used was charcoal, readily available from the great woodlands that covered southern Surrey. Acts of Parliament in Elizabethan times that attempted to pre-serve oak woodland for ship-building made exceptions for the Wealden ironmasters. The frequent protests that iron-working was destroying timber that should be more profit-ably used were exaggerated – it was coppice-wood and the loppings of felled trees that made the best charcoal, not thick timbers. Fuel, indeed, was the most expensive part of the process, accounting for more than half the cost in many cases. Power, on the other hand, was virtually free. The plentiful streams in the area were easily dammed to produce mill-ponds, turning the water-wheels that drove the furnace bellows and the forge hammers. These furnace-ponds and hammer-ponds are the most perma-nent monuments to the industry – those at Abinger Hammer being used as watercress beds today.

Apart from wrought iron, which the blacksmith could make into an endless variety of implements, the cast-iron products of the furnaces included firebacks, cooking-pots, cannon-balls, firedogs, and even grave-slabs. At one Surrey furnace, Imbhams near Chiddingfold, cannons were cast and Boremill Copse nearby records the site of the mill that drilled out the bore of the gun.

The Wealden industry flourished in Tudor and Stuart times, but decline set in as the smelting of iron with cheaper coke in the Midlands made Wealden iron less competitive. Transport on the sticky clay roads had always been diffi-cult and droughts in the early 18th century made water-power unreliable. By 1800 all the ironworks in the Weald of Surrey had disappeared. The slag and cinder is still unearthed from time to time, and the mine-pits and ponds power unreliable. By 1800 all the ironworks in the Weald of Surrey had disappeared. The slag and cinder is still unearthed from time to time, and the mine-pits and ponds remain, often hidden in woods. There are displays at Haslemere Museum relating the history of the Wealden iron industry, including many of the products made when the quiet, rural Weald of Surrey was part of the industrial centre of England.

The
Rotten Borough
of Gatton

PARLIAMENTARY ELECTIONS in Georgian and Regency times were notoriously corrupt and dishonest, and Surrey constituencies were, by and large, no different from others. Few, though, were as obviously unfair as the elections for 'the town and borough of Gatton' – in reality a small estate north-east of Reigate. For 380 years it returned two members to Parliament, as many as the rest of Surrey, excepting the boroughs, and for much of this time there was only one vote cast: that of the owner of the manor of Gatton.

This strange story begins in 1450, when King Henry VI, having given his steward John Tymperley the right to empark his estate at Gatton, apparently also gave him the right to elect two members to each new parliament as if it were a real, populous borough. These privileges were in return for 'his good and faithful services and in consideration of 40 shillings'. It has been suggested that these services rendered by Tymperley were in connection with the King's marriage to Margaret of Anjou in 1444. Whatever they were, Tymperley's reward was magnificent. Not only had he a fashionable hunting-park, but he could 'elect' the two M.P.s himself, for he was the only free-holder of the borough of Gatton. In 1472, in fact, he established a tradition that was to be followed for centuries by electing himself.

However, with the fluctuating fortunes of the Wars of the Roses, Gatton came into the King's hands and royal nominees were returned. In 1540, Henry VIII gave Gatton to his divorced wife Anne of Cleves, who allowed the Copley family to continue living there. The Copleys refused to adopt the Protestant religion at the Reformation, and so when Thomas Copley sat for Gatton in the reign of the Roman Catholic Queen Mary, his views were acceptable. Under Elizabeth, however, matters were different and although he was a distant relative of the Queen by marriage he spent some time in prison for his beliefs. He elected himself to the first three parliaments under Elizabeth, but prison followed and after his release in 1570 Sir Thomas Copley went abroad, where he died in 1584. Thereafter the government, in the person of Elizabeth's formidable minister Lord Burghley, sought to influence the Gatton 'elections' to ensure that the Roman Catholic Lady Copley did not nominate undesirable M.P.s. Lady Copley, however, ignored him and her two choices included her own son – an interesting example of female suffrage in an age long before women had the vote.

It became common practice to use 'pocket' boroughs like Gatton as a means of appointing government-approved members to the House of Commons. Perhaps significantly, two Gatton members were appointed Speaker: Sir John Puckering in 1584 and Sir Thomas Crewe in 1625. The 17th century saw a wind of democracy blowing through Gatton, though, and the franchise was extended to all freeholders in the borough – which amounted to 23. Nevertheless, the owner of Gatton Park continued to dominate the choice of representative. Thomas Turgis, both father and son, sat in every parliament from the

Restoration until the accession of Queen Anne, despite a disputed election in 1660. In 1695 there was a by-election when Turgis's partner was elevated to the House of Lords. This led to the unusual event of votes actually being cast for his successor – eleven for both candidates. This was the sort of deadlock that no amount of recounts could resolve, and in the end George Evelyn was chosen – very probably by the influence of Turgis himself.

The Newland family inherited Gatton in 1703, and they and the Docminiques sat for Gatton unopposed during the first half of the 18th century. In 1751 Sir James Colebrook, a wealthy banker, bought the estate and thereby the borough. On his death ten years later it passed into the hands of his brother. Sir George Colebrook must have had a cynical sense of humour, for in 1765 he had a folly built in the park near his mansion. It was a small Doric temple, supported by columns of cast iron – incidentally, a very early use of this as a building material. This structure was solemnly christened Gatton Town Hall, and the 'elections' were held here. The Latin inscription below an ornamental urn pompously declares 'The well-being of the people is the highest law. ... Let evil deception be absent'. This was, to say the least, tongue-in-cheek. The buying and selling of parliamentary seats like Gatton became an open scandal. It is noticeable that many Gatton M.P.s resigned their places in favour of others – and in fact some resigned because they had also been elected to another constituency as well! There can be no doubt that bribery and government influence were used in these late 18th century elections, which often returned men who had not the remotest connection with Gatton or even Surrey. The power to appoint M.P.s could be very profitably exercised in days when bribery in public life was commonplace. Sir Mark Wood, who purchased Gatton in 1808, was not only an M.P., but also magistrate, churchwarden, overseer of the poor, surveyor of highways, and collector of taxes for the borough. The potential abuse of power thus given to one man enraged radical reformers like William Cobbett, who dismissed Gatton as 'a very rascally spot of earth'.

In 1832 the long-overdue broom of parliamentary reform swept the borough of Gatton into oblivion – indeed, it was quoted as the fourth worst example of its kind in the land. Blechingley, which was hardly better, also lost its M.P.s, as did Haslemere. (Reigate, a notorious sink of bribery, was allowed to keep only one member.) The house that stands in Gatton Park today dates only from 1891, and was almost entirely rebuilt in 1936. Since 1948 it has housed the Royal Alexandra and Albert School, and new buildings cluster now in the park. The Town Hall remains, however. One might almost take it for a tomb or memorial, the last resting place of one of the most rotten of the rotten boroughs of old England.

The Secret Marriage of John Donne

J OHN DONNE (pronounced 'Dunn') was one of the finest
poets of Elizabethan and Jacobean times. He wrote skilfully and passionately in the 'metaphysical' style current at
that time, combining philosophical imagery with intricate
verse-forms. Emotions played as powerful a part in his
life as they did in his poems – and very nearly ruined a
promising career.

John Donne was born in London in 1572 of Roman
Catholic parents, though later he was to become an Anglican after painful and detailed study of the Scriptures. He
went to Oxford at the not unusual age of twelve and then
to Lincoln's Inn to study law eight years later. It is clear
that he was attractive to women, and some of his earlier
poems testify to no little familiarity with physical love. *To
his Mistress going to Bed* is a masterpiece of erotic verse. He
was adventurous as well as amorous, sailing with the Earl
of Essex's fleet against the Spaniards in 1596 and 1597. So
far his career was typical of many a young gentleman of
that time, even to the extent that John Donne lived beyond
his means. What was exceptional in this fashionable and
dashing youth was an ability to use words more skilfully

39

and effectively than others, outstanding even in an age when good English was the rule, rather than the exception. It was this that attracted the attention of the father of two friends of his, Sir Thomas Egerton, Lord Keeper of the Great Seal, and he appointed Donne as his secretary at the end of 1597. Donne more than satisfied the expectations of his employer: 'such a secretary was fitter to serve a king rather than a subject' in Egerton's opinion. The young man's career seemed off to a good start, as the

personal assistant of an influential courtier. It was through Egerton's marriage, however, that a train of events began which was to lead to Donne's prospects being dashed.

Sir Thomas Egerton married Elizabeth, widow of the Surrey landowner Sir John Wolley, in October 1597. She was the sister of Sir George More of Loseley House, near Guildford, who had a large family – including a young daughter Ann. It was perfectly natural for Lady Egerton to bring her niece to London to experience something of court life, and perfectly natural for the fifteen-year-old Ann to meet her step-uncle's secretary. They fell in love. Their meetings had to be kept secret, for they both knew that Sir George More would never let his daughter marry a man with no title or estates – indeed, a man who was hardly more than a servant, no matter how gifted. All his other daughters were wed or betrothed to wealthy landed gentlemen. John and Ann's clandestine courtship came to an abrupt end in 1600, when Lady Egerton died and her niece had to return to Loseley. Before they parted, however, the lovers vowed to be eternally true to each other, even though an arranged marriage for Ann seemed likely.

Nearly two years passed before they met again. Still single, and now seventeen, Ann More returned to London with her father, who had been elected an M.P. for Surrey in the parliament that met in October 1601. Among the other members were Sir Francis Wolley, his sister's son by her first marriage, and John Donne himself. John and Ann consequently met once more and decided that they must marry, whatever the consequences. In December the ceremony was carried out in great secrecy and then Mrs Donne returned with her unsuspecting father to Loseley House.

Clearly, the secret could not be kept for long, but John Donne waited more than a month before he told Sir George, putting off the inevitable for fear of his fiery temper and the knowledge that he personally disliked Donne. There was no right moment to break such news to such a man, however, and when Sir George received a letter from Donne revealing the marriage his fury exceeded the poet's worst fears. Donne's Roman Catholic upbringing, his debts, and his wayward reputation combined to make him an utterly unacceptable son-in-law, despite Donne's insistence that these faults had been exaggerated. Sir George More moved fast. Not only did he have John Donne thrown into prison for marrying a

41

minor without her parent's permission, but he also persuaded his brother-in-law Egerton to sack his secretary. In the event, the courts decided that the marriage was valid, and Sir George had to come to terms with the fact. He grudgingly allowed his daughter to go to live with Donne, but not a single penny of his money went with her. Despite John's pleading, Sir Thomas Egerton refused to re-engage him. Dejectedly, Donne is said to have written to his wife 'John Donne, Ann Donne, undone'.

Indeed, life would have been very black for the couple but for Sir Francis Wolley, Ann's cousin and John's friend. He invited them to live at his house at Pyrford, only nine miles from Loseley. Here Donne studied and wrote poetry, expressing the contentment he felt living with the woman he loved. Ann bore him a daughter in 1603, and that year the new king, James I, visited Pyrford Place. It was an auspicious meeting between the poet and the king, for later James was to befriend Donne. He urged him to enter the church, which he did in 1615 and eventually the King appointed him Dean of St. Paul's. When Ann died in 1617, John suffered the greatest loss of his life, vowing never to marry again – a vow he kept to his own death fourteen years later.

Donne's poetry remains one of the glories of the English language, and although his stay in Pyrford lasted only two or three years it marked a distinct change in his life from a romantic young courtier to a happy and increasingly religious family man. Loseley House still survives, as do the letters he wrote to his angry father-in-law. Pyrford Place has gone, although in the grounds nearby, on the banks of the River Wey stands an old, brick-built summerhouse. Here the poet John Donne was said to have studied and composed his verse, having lost his chances of worldly advancement but gained the happiness of married love.

The Warrior Poets at Farnham Castle

THE EARLY seventeenth century was a golden age of
English poetry. While only a glorious handful equalled
or excelled John Donne, the writing of good verse was an
accomplishment that seemed to come naturally to a high
proportion of the population. Two Surrey gentlemen
attract our attention from amongst this rhyming mul-
titude: John Denham of Egham, whose poem *Cooper's
Hill* has immortalised the locality, and George Wither of
Wanborough, whose forthright and witty *The Manly Heart*
is still regularly published in anthologies. Fate, who enjoys
such ironies, contrived to set them against each other at
Farnham Castle.

The summer of 1642 was a time of tension and distrust.
Zealous supporters of Parliament and dedicated Royalists
were arming themselves for open warfare, while a silent
and gloomy majority looked on helplessly. George Wither
was no passive neutral, though. He had been arguing
Parliament's case against the King in pamphlets and verses,
and when the fighting 'broke out he raised a troop of

43

cavalry. His flag carried the design of a quill pen crossed with a drawn sword, and while the pen may be mightier than the sword, George Wither was going to try both.

Nor was John Denham idle. He set about raising money for the King in the Egham area, and in the middle of October 1642 the King made him Sheriff of Surrey. At the same time Wither was appointed Governor of Farnham Castle by Parliament, under the command of Sir Richard Onslow of Clandon, who had moved rapidly and vigorously to seize Surrey for Parliament's cause. Captain Wither eagerly set to work to fortify the neglected old castle. In his fertile imagination it became the most important stronghold in England, protecting London from the Royalists of the West. He devised grandiose plans for draw-bridges, ramparts, gun emplacements, and all the elaborate defences of 17th century seige warfare. He pestered Onslow to send a military engineer (who presumably would have the expertise to put Wither's fantasies into effect), and also to send cannons, ammunition, men, food, money – an endless list of supplies needed by this vital garrison. However, Sir Richard had other and more pressing concerns. Royalist forces had crossed the Thames and entered north-western Surrey early in November, and Onslow's Surrey Militia were powerless to stop them. All around him Wither felt the increasing hostility of the Farnham people as the Royalists drew nearer. He must have cannon to defend the castle, he decided, and these could only be obtained from Parliament's arsenal in the Tower of London. Onslow had promised guns, but nothing had happened: on the 9th November, with the Royalist tide rising around him, George Wither rode alone to London to beg for them in person. Later he was criticised for leaving his post when it was in such danger, but he tried to justify his ride as a mission to bring help, not a cowardly desertion. In the event, it was futile. The Parliamentarian committee was in a state of panic as reports came in of Royalist advances. They refused to risk valuable artillery in an outpost already doomed, and Wither was ordered to withdraw his men from Farnham. Miserably Wither rode back that night, fearful of an encounter with Royalists known to be in the area. He used waggons and servants from his own estate at Wanborough to carry off the arms and ammunition to Onslow's base at Kingston.

Farnham Castle stood empty for only a few hours. The next day John Denham marched in at the head of the Surrey 'Posse Comitatus', the county force that the Sheriff was empowered to raise to put down disorder. He had with him a hundred men, and even a chaplain, and occupied the castle without opposition. Provisions were needed for the new garrison: it would be poetic justice that the new governor should take them from the old governor. Accordingly the Sheriff's posse descended on Wanborough and plundered Wither's house and estate not only of horses, food, and all kinds of household goods, but also stole his books and writings – something which probably hurt him more.

However, the Royalist tide had reached its highest mark and during November it retreated, leaving Farnham exposed once again, this time to Parliament's armies. On 1st December Sir William Waller, with a small force of cavalry, appeared outside the castle to demand its surrender. Denham refused, as honour demanded. Waller promptly blew in the main gate with a gunpowder charge and his men rushed in. Denham just as promptly surrendered, perhaps rather more readily than honour demanded. He was marched off as a prisoner to London, though he was later released and rejoined the King. George Wither was at this time a Parliamentarian official in Kent, but he returned to Surrey to claim Denham's confiscated estates at Egham as compensation for his losses at Wanborough.

The two poets had much in common and little cause to love each other. Each had plundered the other's home and both had lost Farnham Castle in circumstances that reflected little credit on their courage and military competence. The story is often told that George Wither was at one point taken prisoner and dragged before the King, who would have hanged him if John Denham had not begged for his life. 'While Wither lives' he explained, 'Denham will not be the worst poet in England'. Regrettably, the story cannot be true, for Wither was never captured. Nevertheless, between two men who were skilful poets but less than skilful soldiers, one is entitled to a little poetic licence.

The Great Palace
of Nonsuch

THE SMALL HAMLET of Cuddington stood between Ewell and Cheam; stood, that is, until 1538 when it was swept away to be replaced by a magnificent and extravagantly decorated palace, built by the magnificent and extravagant King Henry VIII. No building anywhere could compare with its splendour – and accordingly it was known as 'Nonsuch'.

Several years and hundred of workmen were required for this ambitious project. Masons, bricklayers, carpenters, and other craftsmen came from all over England and Wales – and specialists from abroad. Bricks and lime for their mortar were fired in kilns on the site, clay and chalk being ready to hand. Timber was freely obtainable from the oak woodlands of Surrey. Suitable stone, however, was less easily acquired. This problem was neatly solved by demolishing Merton Priory and carting the stone rubble to Nonsuch. The Priory had been closed down that same year as part of Henry's Dissolution of the Monasteries and the carved medieval stonework made excellent foundations for the new edifice.

Nonsuch was a typical early Tudor palace in its plan. Basically it consisted of two square courtyards separated by a middle range of buildings. Kitchens, stables, and other domestic buildings stood nearby, and there was an exquisite formal garden, a grove with statues telling the story of Diana and Acteon, and a detached banqueting house. The palace was approached from the London road down an avenue of elms leading to the outer gatetower. As the visitor passed beneath the archway, cleverly-designed acoustic cavities multiplied the echoes of his footsteps. He then found himself in the outer court, faced with stone and battlemented in the prevalent Gothic style.

Around the court were the quarters for the royal servants and courtiers. Ahead was another gatetower, crowned by a clock which chimed the hours. Crossing the outer court, the visitor mounted a short flight of steps and passed through the arch into the inner court. There he stood amazed.

The inner court was a blaze of white and gold: white plaster panels separated by gilded slate covered the walls of the royal apartments. Gods and goddesses, arts and

48

virtues, the labours of Hercules – all were depicted in high relief. While Nonsuch was essentially a Gothic building, this decoration was entirely of the vigorous new Classical style which the Renaissance was spreading throughout Europe. To the right lay the king's quarters, to the left the queen's, and ahead the range which contained the long gallery which linked the two, all sumptuously furnished and ornamented. In the centre of the courtyard splashed a beautiful fountain – where once the old parish church of Cuddington had stood. The drains and foundations of Henry's private quarters cut through the graves of the long dead villagers.

Henry VIII never lived to see his palace completed, although he did visit it two or three times while work was in progress. His son, the boy-king Edward VI stayed once but when Henry's daughter Mary came to the throne she sold Nonsuch to the Earl of Arundel. Soon there was a new Queen of England – the young Elizabeth, and in 1559 Arundel entertained her to an expensive and ostentatious series of feasts and plays at Nonsuch. There was even talk of their marrying. Nothing came of this, however, and the Roman Catholic earl was implicated in plots against the Protestant queen and was imprisoned for a time. Nevertheless, Elizabeth continued to visit Nonsuch, clearly a favourite of hers. This is hardly surprising. Every visitor lavished praise on this remarkable building. Arundel's death in 1580 left his son-in-law with his palace, and his debts. Twelve years later he was obliged to sell Nonsuch to the Queen. It was at her own palace, therefore, that the handsome and ambitious Earl of Essex burst into her bedroom one morning, having returned unbidden from Ireland with perhaps a coup d'etat in mind. He was later to be executed for another attempt to seize power.

After Elizabeth's death in 1603, Nonsuch became the property of Anne, James' queen, and subsequently of Henrietta, wife of Charles I. The royal family often stayed, perhaps hunting in the Little Park around the palace, or in the Great Park to the north of the London road. These happy days came to an end when the Civil Wars began in 1642, and Nonsuch was in Parliamentarian hands in 1648 when a skirmish was fought nearby between the ill-fated Earl of Holland's Royalists and detachments of Cromwell's New Model Army. The Restoration put the amorous Charles II on the throne, and he was to give Nonsuch to one of his mistresses, the Countess of Castlemaine. She had no use for an old-fashioned palace in the country and in 1682 she sold it for the demolition value of its materials to help pay her gambling debts.

The great palace that was the wonder of its age was so thoroughly demolished that even its site was forgotten until an archaeological dig in 1959 revealed its foundations. Some of the finds are now on display at Bourne Hall Museum not far away, but only three small pillars in Nonsuch Park now mark the spot where once stood a palace unrivalled in its day. Truly there was none such.

Guy Fawkes Riots and the Bonfire Boys

BONFIRES HAVE been lit as part of public celebrations in Surrey for centuries, but none more regularly than on the anniversary of the failure of the Gunpowder Plot on the 5th November 1605. In Stuart and Georgian times the church bells were rung (with free beer for the ringers) and special services of thanksgiving held. Bonfires and fireworks were an established feature of the celebrations, so much so that in Godalming in 1768, for example, so many fireworks were being set off in the streets that the constables were ordered to put a stop to it. In this they were unsuccessful, as the custom continued for nearly a hundred years.

By early Victorian times Bonfire Night had become a disorderly and dangerous event in most Surrey market towns, with huge fires being built in main streets. The younger and rougher country people would come in from the villages around, bringing with them anything inflammable to add to the blaze. They were organised by gangs, usually known as the 'Guys' or the 'Bonfire Boys', who wore fancy dress to disguise themselves. Torchlight processions were arranged in many places, headed by a band if one could be obtained, and blazing tar barrels were carried or kicked through the streets. Effigies were paraded and then burnt. Guy Fawkes, of course, usually figured but so also might any unpopular local or national personality who had incurred the dislike of the mob. In 1864 at Farnham, for instance, the Emperor of Austria was burnt for invading Denmark.

Rockets, Roman candles, and 'catten' wheels were set off – but worst of all were the squibs. These were huge home-made bangers, rammed full of gunpowder and powerful enough to blow in a window; the most fearful type was known as a 'serpent', a giant jumping-jack that could fly over a house. Those who lived in the town centres had to shutter their windows and cover up their cellar-gratings to stop the fireworks from getting in. Increasingly in the middle of the last century the mob took advantage of their numbers – and the fact they could not be recognised in disguise – to pay back grudges against unpopular local figures. Perhaps the worst excesses were at Guildford.

The Guildford Guys were a well-organised secret society, and were said to number amongst them the sons of respectable tradesmen and gentry as well the rougher elements of the town. They seemed curiously safe from prosecution and were certainly never short of money for their festivities, whether their own, or contributions solicited from townsmen too afraid of reprisals to refuse. For days beforehand fireworks were made and disguises prepared, and as the night fell on the 5th November the Guys came to town. As they paraded in, they uttered their eerie rallying cries – 'Loo! Loo!' or 'Phillaloo muster!' – and brought cartloads of fuel with them. The traditional site for the bonfire was at the top of the High Street between Holy Trinity and Abbot's Hospital, and soon the flames would be leaping up. The ringleaders of the 'Guys Society' would issue orders by means of a horn and more fuel would be added from time to time. Gates, fencing, doors – anything to hand would be uprooted and thrown on the blaze. On one occasion the grandstand at Merrow racecourse was pulled down and on another a four-wheeled van was pushed onto the fire to the cheers of the onlookers – which included the owner of the van until he realised it was his. The squibs shattered the air and the mob ruled. The authorities seemed reluctant to interfere. The police were too few to cope, and the Head Constable would lock his men safely in the police station with bread, cheese, and beer to last them until the morning. If the Mayor or any other official had spoken out against the Guys then he could expect to have his windows broken on the night, if nothing worse.

Throughout the 1850s matters got more and more out of hand. Attempts by the Surrey Constabulary and the Guildford Borough Police to intervene were overwhelmed. On one occasion the unfortunate policemen were ambushed on their way to put out a decoy fire on the Mount by the Guys, who were lying in wait in the alleyways over the Town Bridge. Driven back by volleys of stones, the retreating officers barricaded themselves into the county Police Station in Woodbridge Road while the jeering mob smashed the windows. By 1863 the Guys were also putting in their unwelcome appearance at other national celebrations in the town and eventually the Corporation decided that enough was enough. They elected Philip Jacob as Mayor for as long as it would take him to put an end to the Guys' rioting. Troops were called in, special constables sworn, and the police were issued with cutlasses. These patrolled the town from the 5th November until the 21st, when the soldiers were withdrawn. Two hours after they marched out, the Guys marched in. They proceeded to wreak vengeance on those who had frustrated them. A patrolling policeman, P.C. Sutton, was seized and thrown on the bonfire, escaping with serious burns. The mayor had to be roused from his bed to read the Riot Act from the Guildhall balcony and at other points, after which the town quietened down. The following Bonfire Night in

1864 passed with little activity, as it also did in the next year. The last – and potentially the most serious fling of the Guys came, however, on Boxing Day 1865. A disguised gang attacked P.C. Stent in the High Street, clubbing him to the ground. A strong party of police with cutlasses drawn came running to the rescue and after a vicious struggle arrested four of the mob. These young workmen, all in their twenties, were sent to prison. From then on no more was heard of the Guildford Guys.

In common with many Surrey towns, the disorderly town-centre bonfire in Guildford was replaced by an officially-organised one outside the town, and this continues today in Stoke Park. One would have to go to Lewes or Battle in Sussex to recapture the flavour of the old Bonfire Nights.

The Persecution
of the
Godstone Martyrs

ONE OF THE darkest shadows that is cast across the history of the Church is the willingness of Christians to kill other Christians of whose particular brand of Christianity they disapprove. The persecution of heretics in the name of the God of Love is a mournful and unedifying spectacle, but one which has been witnessed all too often. Perhaps it is understandable, if not pardonable, because whatever people care deeply about they are prepared to kill for – and be killed. Under the Tudors hundreds of English men and women were executed for their adherence to the Roman church, the Anglican church, or to personal religious doctrines that neither church would tolerate. Two such were John Launder and Thomas Iveson of Godstone.

John Launder, a farm labourer, was 25 when he travelled to Brighton on some business for his father at the end of October 1554. Mary Tudor had been on the throne for over a year, and was attempting to restore the Roman form of Christianity which had been swept away in the

Reformation of Henry VIII's and Edward VI's time. Many had died in those days rather than abandon the old religion, and there were many who welcomed the return of the Latin services and the banning of the English prayer book. Nevertheless, John Launder remained loyal to the Protestant way of worship, as did his friend Thomas Iveson, a Godstone carpenter who had also made the journey to Brighton. While they were there, they learnt that a local brewer, Dirick or Derek Carver, was holding services using the English prayer book in his own home. These were attended by those who refused to go to the parish church where the Latin service was used. John and Thomas went to Carver's house, despite the risk of being arrested.

There were those in the neighbourhood who resented such heretical meetings, however, and someone informed the authorities. A local magistrate and his constables burst into the brewer's house while the small congregation was at prayer, and arrested Launder, Iveson, and Carver. They were sent up to London, where they were examined by the Queen's council before being committed to Newgate Prison. There they waited for seven months before they received the inevitable summons to appear before Bishop Bonner.

Edmund Bonner, Bishop of London, was a dedicated persecutor of heretics and personally condemned more than any other prelate in Mary's reign. His trials were conducted on a standard pattern and when on 8th June 1555 John Launder and Thomas Iveson were brought to his house, they were interrogated about their religious beliefs. They had to sign statements of their opinions about certain key theological issues, and the fact that they could both sign their names suggests that they were better educated than most Surrey labourers or tradesmen at that time. The Bishop objected to some of their opinions. Amongst other points, John Launder considered that confession to a priest was unnecessary, and that at the

Communion the bread and wine was not actually transformed into Christ's flesh and blood. This, and other Protestant doctrines, he had believed since he was about 18, and had been used to defending them in discussions in his native Godstone.

Bonner's patient but determined attempts to persuade him that he was mistaken accordingly fell on deaf ears. Launder retorted 'I will never go from these answers as long as I live'. Thomas Iveson's attitudes were similar to Launder's and he too refused to be swayed by the Bishop's threats and pleadings. Bonner then dismissed them, allowing them a day to think things over in prison before calling them to appear before his diocesan court at St. Paul's. Here their answers were read out, and they were asked if they still maintained their doctrines to be true. Iveson replied 'I would not recant and forsake my opinion and belief for all the goods in London'. The court once more tried to get them to change their minds, for the churchmen sincerely wished the pair to live as theologically-sound Roman Catholics rather than die and be damned as heretics.

All was in vain. Both obstinately refused to alter their statements, and so both were condemned. As was the normal practice, the diocesan court handed the pair over to the secular authorities for punishment, with a plea that this should not be too severe. This plea was merely conventional, however: everybody concerned knew the fate that was in store for Launder and Iveson. On 23rd July 1555 John Launder was burned at the stake at Steyning in Sussex and Thomas Iveson at Chichester at about the same time. Perhaps these places were chosen so that their dreadful deaths would be more widely known than simply in their own village. Both were true to their word. Neither altered any of their opinions to the end.

The deaths of the Godstone martyrs and others like them did much to create hostility between Roman Catholics and Protestants, and when Anglicanism returned with

Queen Elizabeth, revenge was exacted. It was then the turn of many Roman Catholics to follow Launder and Iveson along the painful path of martyrdom, such as John Felton of Bermondsey in Surrey, burned at St. Paul's in 1570, and his son Thomas, hanged for wanting to become a priest. The legacy of bitterness has taken many years to fade, indeed perhaps in an increasingly secular society tolerance has grown because indifference to religion has grown. In some ways it would be better to forget the Godstone martyrs and the Feltons, so that their memories should not stir up once more the fires of antagonism. Nevertheless, their moral stands and deaths are an unalterable, if deplorable, part of Surrey's history and should remind us that opinions different from our own can be equally sincerely held and equally worth dying for.

The Golden Years of Brooklands

In 1906 THE INFANT British motor industry was being hampered by a lack of government encouragement – a 20 m.p.h. speed limit was an example of this. Hugh Locke King decided that a purpose-built motor racetrack was needed, a place where British cars could develop performances to match or better their Continental rivals. He set out to build just such a circuit on his estate at Weybridge. It was to become famous, not only as the cradle of the British motor industry but also as the birthplace of British aviation, under the simple but magic name of Brooklands.

Work was scarce in that winter and hundreds of Yorkshire navvies came to work on the site for 6d an hour. The $2\frac{3}{4}$ mile embankment was built of rammed sand, with a six-inch surface of concrete. Locke King personally supervised the work, which was completed in the creditably short time of eight months, opening on 17th June 1907. The racetrack was an immediate success. Not only cars raced: bicycles also whizzed around the steeply-curved embankment that year, and motorcycles soon after. Perhaps more significantly, in December 1907 the young engineer A. V. Roe began constructing and testing his bamboo, wood, and canvas aeroplane in a shed near the judges' box. His pioneering experiments in manned flight laid the foundations of the British aircraft industry, and a plaque near the Clubhouse today commemorates his achievements. Vickers, the Sheffield steelmakers, set up a flying school at Brooklands in 1912 and others followed suit. As Locke King had hoped, the motor circuit became a powerful stimulus to technical development – streamlining was soon recognised as essential for fast racing cars, for example – and British prestige in international motor sport was in the ascendant. These advances were not made without cost, however. In 1913 Percy Lambert was killed in his record-breaking 25 h.p. Talbot during another record attempt. The story is told that his ghost still walks at Brooklands, dressed in helmet and goggles, while it is said that the sound of an old racing car can be heard late at night driving round the track – a track which today is no longer a complete circuit.

The outbreak of the First World War in 1914 brought an end to racing at Brooklands, but the beginning of large-scale aircraft production. Vickers set up a factory there in 1915, making military biplanes. The design department was equipped with one of the earliest wind-tunnels in the world. A Vickers Vimy heavy bomber was the first aeroplane to fly the Atlantic, in the year after the war ended, and it was developed into one of the first commercial airliners.

The end of the war saw the return of the racers. The advanced development of aero-engines for military purposes also benefited racing-car design, and speeds rapidly increased. The first British Grand Prix was held in 1926, but the small, family car was also catered for: the little Austin Seven made its reputation at Brooklands. Motorcycling also came back with the return of peace – a peace that was shattered by the roar of powerful vee-twin engines, like that of the American Harley-Davidson which was the first to break the 100 m.p.h. barrier for a motorcycle in Britain. The economic recession of the late 1920s led to fewer professional riders and more amateurs risking the thrills and the inevitable spills. Meanwhile, the cars regularly raised the lap record for the circuit, culminating in Cobb's astonishing average speed of 143 m.p.h. in 1935. However, the steeply-banked circuit at Brooklands was already becoming obsolete. Built when suspensions were bad and speeds comparatively low, it had been an effective way of keeping the cars on the track. Now such banking had become unnecessary, and level race-tracks were more practical. Despite this, when war again broke out in 1939 and racing ceased, few realised that this time it had ceased for good.

As in 1914, the interruption of peacetime racing was a sign for redoubled effort on the part of the aircraft manufacturers. The Hawker Hurricane had first taken to the air at Brooklands in 1935, and Vickers' brilliant designer, Barnes Wallis, had been developing the Wellington bomber, with its revolutionary 'geodetic' lattice construction. Over 2,500 Wellingtons were built at Brooklands during the war

– one, which crashed into Loch Ness in 1940, has been salvaged and returned to its birthplace. The Germans were not unaware of the importance of Brooklands, and bombed the Vickers works in September 1940, causing many casualties. The increased output demanded by the war required an expansion of the works, and hangars were built on the home straight of the race track. More drastically, part of the embankment was dug out to build another hangar, thus effectively destroying the track as a circuit.

After the war it became clear that racing was no longer viable at Brooklands and the track was sold to Vickers in 1946. Barnes Wallis and his research and development team moved into the old Clubhouse, and continued work on such projects as the 'swing-wing', which was to bear fruit many years later in aircraft like Concorde and the Tornado. Post-war Vickers' airliners included the Viscount, the Vanguard, and the VC10. Vickers became part of the British Aircraft Corporation in 1964 and British Aerospace in 1977, and still occupies the original site. Barnes Wallis retired at the age of 84 in 1971, and died eight years later. Two of the huge bombs he designed during the war are now displayed alongside a Wellington bomber in one of the hangars.

Perhaps the most exciting museum project in Surrey today is the Brooklands Museum, based in the old Clubhouse and displaying aircraft, motor vehicles and other items associated with this remarkable site, which has contributed so much to transport by land and air.

Lord Lyttleton's Death

THOMAS LORD LYTTLETON lived the life of a self-indulgent rake, typical of too many of the aristocracy in Georgian times. If his life was deplorable, it was unexceptional. His death, however, was surrounded with such singular circumstances as to arouse astonishment, dread, and perhaps a little self-righteous satisfaction.

The story begins in Worcestershire, where Lord Lyttleton began to pay increasing attention to three young and beautiful sisters who lived with their recently widowed mother nearby. The mother, Mrs. Amphlett, was a strict and religious gentlewoman and his reputation was such as to make her view his advances to her daughters with apprehension. He persisted, though, and on New Year's Day 1779 he sent the three girls expensive presents. (It was then the custom to give presents at New Year, rather than Christmas.) He enclosed a letter couched in Biblical terms, exhorting the young ladies to high moral behaviour and to follow the example of their pious mother. It is uncertain whether this ingratiating letter convinced Mrs. Amphlett of Lyttleton's honourable motives, but her worst fears were soon to be realised. By the summer the three girls – aged fifteen, seventeen and nineteen – were living with Lyttleton in his country house. In September he visited Ireland, taking Christianna with him and leaving Elizabeth and Margaret at his home. Their mother was frantic with worry about them, and even more so when her daughters went to stay at Lyttleton's town house in London on his return to England a month later. It was common gossip that he had seduced all three.

On the morning of the 25th November 1779 Lord Lyttleton came down to breakfast a worried man. He told the others of the house party, which included Lord Fortescue, Lady Flood, and Captain Wolseley as well as the Misses Amphlett, that he had had a dream. A bird had fluttered into his bedroom, he said, and then had changed into the figure of a woman, who told him to prepare to depart this world and join her in the other. 'I hope not soon' cried the fearful lord. 'Yes, in three days', replied the apparition – and vanished.

The assembled company made light of the story, and reminded Lord Lyttleton of an incident earlier in the week when a robin had flown into the room where he was. The dream was surely just a memory of that. He remained depressed and deeply troubled, nevertheless, and to prevent him from brooding upon it, the ladies suggested that the following day they should all go to Epsom, where Lord Lyttleton owned Pitt Place, a house near the church, which he had won as a gambling debt. The fashionable gaiety of Epsom was such as to put the whole party in high spirits, and even Lyttleton himself tried to put a brave face on his worries. He had survived two days, he said, and if he could live beyond midnight on the third he would have 'bilked' or 'jockeyed' the ghost – meaning 'cheated' in the gambler's slang of the time.

All went reasonably well until the third evening, although he did have an attack of the choking fits which he suffered from time to time. This was nothing unusual, however, and later that night the three young ladies, possibly not for the first time, 'accompanied his Lordship to his room to notice some paintings'. The Misses Amphlett then went to bed and Lord Lyttleton called his valet to prepare to retire himself. There are conflicting accounts as to what happened next. Some have Lyttleton confidently ordering his breakfast for the morning, others say that he sent the servant out of the room to fetch a teaspoon to stir up the medicine the physician had prescribed for his fits. What is certain, however, is that a severe attack of choking seized the lord as he sat up in bed. Later the valet was to say that Lord Lyttleton died in his arms; others maintain that the panic-stricken servant rushed out calling for help rather than assisting his master. In any event, Lord Lyttleton was soon dead. And it was still a little before midnight.

The sensation caused by his death was heightened by reports that arrived telling of the death of Mrs. Amphlett at the exact moment when Lyttleton had seen his vision. She had died, they said, of despair and grief at the ruin of her daughters. The story of what had happened at Pitt Place spread rapidly, and in the nature of these things, it gained much in the telling. Conflicting and contradictory versions appeared, with exaggerations and extravagant detail. Some maintained that at the precise time he died, Lyttleton's ghost itself appeared to a friend who had long accompanied him in his wicked and dissolute life – afterwards this friend would never stay at Pitt Place when he visited, but always insisted on sleeping at the Spread Eagle in the town. Another version of the story has the house-party staying up with Lyttleton on that fateful evening, turning all the clocks on to pass the dreaded hour of midnight the sooner. Lord Westcote, who was Lyttleton's uncle, related the story to Samuel Johnson: the old sage remarked 'I am glad to have evidence of the spiritual world'.

Disregarding the inconsistencies and contradictions in the different versions of the affair, all agree that Lord Lyttleton was genuinely disturbed by his dream and did die three nights later. Whether this depression predisposed him to a fatal seizure, whether it was merely a coincidence, or whether some supernatural power really did intervene it would be presumptuous to say.

The Tragic
Figure of
Billy Hicks

THE POWER of human love is such as to raise those it ensnares to the heights of exultation and yet also plunge them into the depths of despair. A love that is rejected or frustrated is a burden only the strongest can bear without bending or breaking. For the weaker it can be an intolerable misery. Few, though, can have suffered more than Billy Hicks. Unfulfilled love robbed him of his reason, ruined his life, and ultimately saw him die a wretched and derided outcast.

William Hicks was born in 1780 of a respectable and well-established Surrey family. In his youth he seems to have shown some of the eccentricity that was later to characterise his life by insisting on being apprenticed to a miller at Steep in Hampshire. This would indeed be eccentric in a young gentleman, with a good education and the assurance of a respectable income. It may, however, have been a ploy to bring him closer to a working-class girl there with whom he had fallen deeply in love. When William's parents came to know of it, they were furious. She was no fitting match for their only son of whom they had higher hopes. They accordingly did everything in their power to hinder the affair. William would at this time have been in his late teens – a sensitive and emotional age and one when he was still legally in the power of his parents. When he finally asked them for their consent to marry his love, they flatly refused.

Whether William was emotionally unstable by nature or whether his character was unable to withstand this blow will never be known. Suffice it to say that from that day onwards it became increasingly clear that his mind had become unhinged. He gradually degenerated from a country gentleman into a bitter and anti-social tramp, living in the worst conceivable bachelor squalor. He never seems to have considered marrying any other woman – in the days when any woman might consider him – nor is it recorded whether he attempted to marry his sweetheart when he came of age (possibly she had already married another). In due course he inherited his parents' wealth

and for a time was seen around Shere riding a well-bred hunter and dressed as befitted a man of his social position. He took to frequenting racing meetings and probably gambled away much of his inheritance. At Ascot races in the 1820s his increasingly erratic behaviour led him to throw his hat at King George. This was inevitably followed by his arrest, and he was sentenced to nine months in the House of Correction at Guildford. The hat was never returned to him, and Billy Hicks resented this for years afterwards, as a local poet noted:

> At Ascot Heath in years gone by
> At George the Fourth he threw
> His hat and on his own bald head
> The royal vengeance drew.
> Within old Guildford's prison walls
> Nine months he spent for that;
> And evermore he styled great George
> The thief that stole his hat.

Not only bald but growing obese and dirty in his personal habits, Billy Hicks found himself repeatedly at odds with the authorities as his behaviour grew more aggressive. He spent a year in prison after assaulting a man and refusing to be bound over to keep the peace. He obstinately rejected offers of help from his friends – for at that time he still had friends.

In the early 1830s he moved into a miserable and filthy hovel at Shere, where he was to live for the rest of his unhappy life. He washed his clothes in the Tillingbourne nearby; washed them, that is, on the rare occasions that he gave himself that trouble. He spent his time aimlessly wandering the country lanes with a dog, a goat, and a donkey pulling a ramshackle cart. He still had enough money left, however, to have kept him in comfort if not luxury if he had so wished, but that was not the life he chose. In one of his wilder fits he cut off his donkey's ears and tail – an act of irrational brutality for which he was once more put in prison. The donkey nevertheless remained a faithful companion of his for the rest of his life, despite the cruel mutilation it had suffered at his hands.

This strange and aimless procession became a familiar part of the scene in central Surrey, the gross and slovenly Billy Hicks seated on his donkey, pulling its cart, with the dog and the goat trotting on either side. The heartless and vindictive cruelty natural to gangs of small boys made Billy an object of derision and persecution. He was continually jeered at and pelted with stones – though a dangerous victim, for he soundly beat any of his tormentors he could catch. One day he was meandering homewards from Guildford, having attended the races on Merrow Downs, when some schoolboys threw stones, one of which hit him on the head. His dog instantly leapt on the culprit and held him tightly until his master could lumber over. The dog then stood by to witness the punishment with evident satisfaction.

Billy Hicks seems to have inspired the loyalty of his animals, though not of human kind. Old and rejected, a grotesque figure of fun, he committed suicide in his squalid home in 1854 – a suicide, one might think, that had been foreshadowed for fifty years or more. He left a not inconsiderable sum of money to his sister's children, perhaps the only mortals for whom he had any affection. It is quite impossible to say whether his fate would have been any different if he had been able to marry the girl he loved all those years ago. Nevertheless, his sad and wasted life emphasises just how narrow a divide there may be between contentment and despair.

Morris Dancing
and
May Day Revels

THE JINGLING BELLS and waving handkerchiefs of the Morris men are an evocative part of the rural scene and the growth in the number of Morris sides in the last ten or fifteen years has made their dancing a familiar sight throughout the country. It is often claimed that the Morris is a remnant of an ancient fertility rite. A good story, but one that does not square with the historical records. It seems more likely that it derives from a late medieval court dance that spread to the towns and then the villages. Surrey, like most parts of England, had a strong local tradition of Morris dancing from Henry VII's days until mid-Victorian times when, like so much of the traditional way of life, it was submerged beneath the suburban culture of the incomers.

At first Morris dancing, having left the court, became associated with the annual festivities organised to raise money for parish purposes. This has left some interesting records in churchwarden's accounts. In 1509–10, for example, the parish of Kingston-upon-Thames provided six pairs of shoes 'for ye mores daunsers' and six years later nine named men were again provided with shoes. Presumably dancing was as hard on shoe-leather then as it is now. The parish seems actually to have owned the Morris dancers' costumes. In 1530 the parish of Holy Trinity in Guildford was hiring out its Morris gear. A painting of the Thames at Richmond, dating from the 1620s, shows the kind of spectacle provided at that date: four men, one of them dressed as a woman, dance to the music of a pipe and tabor while a fool or jester collects from the onlookers.

The seventeenth and eighteenth centuries provide few surviving records of Morris dancing in Surrey, but it clearly continued to be a familiar part of country life. For example, John Russell, a Guildford tradesman in Georgian times, lists Morris bells among the dozens of items he has in stock.

The virtuoso execution of solo dances or 'jigs' was a recognised accomplishment in west Surrey by the early 1800s. The curate of Puttenham, writing in 1869, noted that 'Puttenham like most other places had its morris dancers in former times – but none of the present generation remember having seen the performers with bells, as was the ancient practice. But Mr. Fludder states that Thomas Furlonger his father's carter wore them in the dance, and that he was by far the best dancer in the whole neighbourhood, the bells on his legs and ankles keeping wonderful time with the musician. Master Strudwick was one of the most famous of the modern school, though he danced without the bells' ... and after walking the 35 miles from Puttenham, outdanced a Cockney in London.

In the middle of the last century the Morris was an important part of the chimneysweeps' May Day revels. In 1935 it was recorded that 'one old Kingstonian ... remembers when as a boy he and seven others, with "Jack in Green" and a piper who also beat a drum, dressed themselves up and went about the town "gigging" on May Day. They went from house to house and did simple traditional dances which he learned from the others. A lady remembers that the dancers were dressed up fantastically and had long waving streamers and coloured ribbons from their hats and costumes, and that they had a man with them who played a pipe and beat a drum, while they danced around the maypole, and did jerky dances which the people called gigs.'

John Mason, once Mayor of Guildford, recalls the town in the 1830s and 1840s. 'May Day was the chimney sweepers' holiday. They then dressed in suits after the manner of a harlequin, tinselled and spangled in all the colours of the rainbow, and in groups of five or six performed their peculiar dance, beating out the tune to the music of the shovel and brush and triangle.' George Sturt, the Farnham wheelwright, remembers the sweeps coming round on May Day in the 1860s: 'they sang and danced, clattering their wooden shovels and one of them "playing the bones" held between his knuckles. ... Yet though they were bedecked with ribbons and laughed and made merry, the merriment was rather obviously "made".'

Regrettably, no detailed description of the sweeps' dances, or the Morris men's jigs survives from Surrey. When Cecil Sharp, the folksong collector, began to note down Morris dances at the beginning of this century, he concentrated on the Cotswold area and ignored the south east. Accordingly, with the revival of Morris dancing in later years, the Cotswold style became the most widespread. For example, Miss Musgrave of Hascombe started a Morris side among the local schoolchildren in 1911 after corresponding with Cecil Sharp. The costumes they wore and the dances they performed were all copied from Oxfordshire and Warwickshire originals. It is clear that by this time the old Surrey Morris had been forgotten.

Between the wars a few Morris sides were established in Surrey, and a number in the years following the last war, but the majority of sides dancing today were formed in the late 1960s or early 1970s in what might be described as a Morris boom. This has also seen the advent of women dancers, looked upon with some disapproval by some as it is untraditional, and the introduction of styles of dancing other than that of the Cotswolds – the clog dances of Lancashire and Cheshire, in particular. Indeed, there are probably more people dancing the Morris in Surrey today than there ever had been in the past. Sadly, though, none dance the old local dances, for these have irrevocably departed into the darkness of our unrecorded past.

Matthew Trigg
and the
Ash Church Steeple

THERE SEEMS to have been a widespread impulse to explain any feature the origin of which was unknown by a fanciful tale. Strange mounds or crevices were blamed on the Devil, or the fairies, or even Oliver Cromwell, and such disparate facts as the old cauldron which undoubtedly lay in Frensham church and the cave which unquestionably existed at Moor Park gave rise to the tale of Mother Ludlam the witch. Similarly at Aldershot there were two aspects of local life which were held to have a single and most singular explanation. There was a dent in the church spire at Ash, two miles away, and old Matthew Trigg walked with a limp.

Aldershot in the 1700s – before the coming of the great army camps in the middle of the next century – was a tiny and somewhat impoverished hamlet among the infertile heathland of the Surrey–Hampshire border. The inhabitants were so few, and so familiar with each other that they were soon aware when one of their number, Matthew Trigg, suddenly and mysteriously disappeared. Search parties were organised and scoured the bracken-clad heaths around – but to no avail. After much fruitless

74

seeking and enquiring, the villagers gathered to discuss what next to do. The only suggestion which had any hope of success was to consult a noted 'wise man' and this was

agreed upon. It was well known that such folk were gifted with the power to locate lost or stolen property – so why not people as well?

Accordingly the wizard was consulted and at length gave his answer. Matthew Trigg, he declared, had been spirited away by the 'pharisees' or fairies, and was now among them far away to the east (presumably deep in Surrey, or even Kent – a county of which most of the villagers would have heard but few have visited). The villagers were not to worry, however: the wise man knew how to free him from his enchanted captivity and return him to his friends and relations. This he did by summoning up a flying horse. Whether or not this had the splendid wings of Pegasus (often seen around Aldershot to this day) is left to the imagination of the reader.

In any event, this supernatural horse flew up into the air and set off towards the east. Unerringly it flew on until it came to where Matthew Trigg stood amongst a group of the fairies and landed by his side. The pharisees were impressed by the beautiful and magical creature, and tried to catch it. The horse easily eluded their grasp, however, and Matthew Trigg was able to scramble up onto its back. Up soared the splendid animal into the air and turned back westwards. Over the North Downs they flew, heedless of ditches and hedges, skimming over the treetops and farmhouses below, while Matthew clung grimly on. He tried to control his magical mount – whether it simply refused to answer the reins or whether it had no saddle or bridle at all the story does not relate. Suffice it to say that the horse flew in a line straight as an arrow towards Aldershot, following the ground at a constant height of some fifty or sixty feet.

This, as it turned out, was unfortunate. As they neared their goal, Matthew realised they were heading for the spire of Ash church, lying directly in their path. No heaving or squeezing or shouting on his part could get the horse to deviate its course around the obstacle or rise over it. The inevitable happened. Horse and rider struck the lead-covered spire a glancing blow that shook it to its foundations. The owls that lived in the tower flew out screeching, and the spire was left irretrievably bent. Poor Matthew's knee was badly injured by the impact, but the horse was evidently unhurt. It fulfilled its mission dutifully and deposited the man back in his home village, where his friends helped him to dismount and treated his injury, glad at least to have him back alive. Matthew Trigg was no doubt glad himself to be back among humankind, but even after his knee had healed he walked with a limp for the rest of his long life.

Of course, if anyone who heard this tale cast doubt upon its truth and demanded proof, it was only necessary to point out lame old Matthew Trigg as he limped past, and show the doubter the bend in the steeple at Ash. Or rather, this could have been done while Trigg lived and the Ash steeple stood. However, in 1864 the wealthy and generous rector of Ash, Gilbert Heathcote, had the old small spire replaced with the present larger one when the church was substantially rebuilt. The new one was, as a matter of course, completely straight. Now that Matthew Trigg himself has long ago limped once more out of the mortal world – this time permanently – there is nothing left to substantiate the tale. In the absence of any real evidence as to its origins, I would suggest it began as an entertaining yarn in the locality and became something of a minor legend in western Surrey. How seriously anyone took such tales at the time is impossible to know, but they served a purpose of a kind, if only to give some slight supernatural thrill to what otherwise would be merely commonplace and everyday things.

Gertrude Jekyll and Old West Surrey

G ERTRUDE JEKYLL (pronounced to rhyme with 'treacle') was born in London in 1843, but moved with her family to Bramley in Surrey at the age of 4½. She grew into something of a tomboy, but when her brothers went to boarding-school, she was left to her own devices. Wandering the lanes around her home, the little girl made friends with the country people – relishing the clean scent of the carpenter's wood-shavings, fishing in the Wey and Arun Canal with the wharfinger, or admiring the horse-brasses at the saddler's. She came to know and love the life of the villagers, their cottages and gardens, in what she was later to name Old West Surrey.

Gertrude was primarily an artist, and when she was 18 she enrolled at the Kensington School of Art. She travelled abroad, and became an admirer of the painter G. F. Watts. Her family moved to Berkshire in 1869, but Gertrude still mingled in the artistic circles of her day, meeting John Ruskin and possibly also the influential William Morris, a leading Pre-Raphaelite. After her father's death in 1876, the family moved back to west Surrey, at Munstead Heath. The building of a separate house for Gertrude was prompted by the continual comings and goings of her 'arty' friends.

However glad Gertrude Jekyll was to return to Surrey,

she soon became aware that the way of life she had loved in her childhood was fast becoming obliterated as in-comers, mostly from London, began to build and settle in the country. She was determined to rescue or record as much as she could of the old rural life, and in the years that followed she toured the area west of Dorking and south of the Downs, collecting old cottage furnishings and photographing not only the cottages and their gardens, but the cottage-dwellers themselves. In this she was ahead of her time. While others had deplored the changes that resulted from the railway's opening-up of backward rural areas, Gertrude Jekyll actually did something about it. She made a detailed record in words, pictures, and objects of the country-folk's clothing, speech, habits, and work as well as their homes and gardens. Sadly, much of the furn-ishings and utensils she acquired were bought at sales when old cottages were cleared for newcomers – cheap, manufactured furniture replaced the craftsman's oak, oil-lamps replaced the rushlights, iron kitchen ranges replaced cooking on the open 'down hearths'.

In 1889 she met the young architect Edwin Lutyens at Littleworth, and so began the working relationship that was to last the rest of her life. She brought an artist's eye for colour and form to the design of gardens for the houses which Lutyens planned: 'living pictures with land and trees and flowers'. When in 1891 her eye-specialist told her to give up fine work like her painting and em-broidery, she devoted herself to gardens as an expression of her creativity. Inspired by the cottage gardens of old west Surrey, her work perfecty complemented Lutyens' use of local stone, timber, and tile in the 'vernacular' tradition. Lutyens himself designed a new house for Gertrude Jekyll at Munstead Wood, which was completed in 1897. It is an especially good example of the way Lutyens employed local materials and techniques – 'sound work done with the right intention' in Gertrude's words.

Her collaboration with Lutyens soon brought fame to

them both, and 'a Lutyens house with a Jekyll garden' became an established part of the English scene. Her books and articles on gardening were influential, although like the ideas of most great designers in less skilful hands they were often debased. The standardised privet hedges and herbaceous borders of so many 20th century suburbs derive from an uninspired interpretation of her work, just as the uniform rows of semi-detached houses had planks nailed to their brickwork as a crude gesture towards the timber-framing so deftly employed by Lutyens.

A landmark in English social history was the publication in 1904 of her book *Old West Surrey*, in which she details the country life of her childhood and castigates landowners who were 'robbing England of so much of her priceless heritage of simple beauty'. In 1907 Gertrude Jekyll presented her collection of cottage byegones to the Surrey Archaeological Society at Guildford, where a new museum gallery was built to display it in 1911. She continued to design gardens, many of them in west Surrey, until her death in 1932. She is buried in the family grave in the churchyard of St. John's, Busbridge. The epitaph is simple: 'Gertrude Jekyll – artist, gardener, craftswoman'. One might fairly add 'pioneer social historian'.

It is the lot of garden designers to see their work alter and perhaps disappear as the seasons pass, unless a conscious effort is made to preserve the original concept. Few Jekyll gardens are now exactly as she planned them, and few examples of her painting and other craftwork survive. However, a display of her folk-life collection may be seen at Guildford Museum, and the National Trust has restored Oakhurst Cottage at Hambledon as a meticulously-recreated home of the kind she so clearly described. Indeed, some of the items on display there are from her own collection, and Oakhurst Cottage has become something of a shrine to the vanished country life that Gertrude Jekyll loved as a child in Old West Surrey.

Contraband and the Smuggling Heathers

THE HIGH LAND between Ewhurst and Shere has little to offer the farmer. The sandy, infertile soils support birch and bracken, however, and also the hurts – known elsewhere as whortleberries or bilberries – which give their name to the Hurtwood. Heath also thrives in these inhospitable uplands and this, too, lent its name in days past to the wild, lawless inhabitants of the heathland – the Heathers.

The Heathers (pronounced 'Heethers') had a bad reputation. They could not earn a living honestly in the woodlands where they built their squatters' cottages. The dwellers in the valleys below, in Shere and Gomshall, in Cranleigh and Ewhurst, viewed them with unconcealed suspicion for being a Heather. Peaslake, no more than a scattered hamlet in those days, was the nearest thing to a village in the Hurtwood, and until the narrow lanes were improved in Victorian times the whole areas was largely cut off from the rest of Surrey. No wonder, then, if poachers and petty thieves found it a safe refuge from the law; and no wonder if the settled farming folk around feared them. A young girl in Ewhurst in the early years of the last century saw smoke rising one evening from an abandoned cottage on the hillside above her home. She knew that 'the Peaslake men were having a night of it', roasting a stolen pig, or chickens, perhaps, and the whole family lay trembling in their beds.

The crime in which the Heathers were suspected of being most deeply involved was smuggling – indeed, if it was called a crime in old Surrey. Many, perhaps most, people in 18th century England considered the high import duties on tea, brandy, and other luxury goods to be iniquitous. The smugglers were more often thought of as 'free traders' (the name they always called themselves) than as criminals.

Smugglers were divided into two distinct groups: the seamen and the landsmen. The seamen were specialists, not only in the exacting technicalities of handling vessels under sail but also in the skills needed to evade the Revenue cutters and land their cargoes undetected. It was here that the landsmen took over, 'running' the contraband goods to their final market – a market which included many of the most wealthy and influential people in the land. This being so, the principal destination was London, and one of the established routes from the coast west of Shoreham ran through the Hurtwood.

The landsmen needed just as much specialist knowledge as the seamen, for they had to know the countryside well enough to be able to lead their pack-ponies through side-roads and tracks in the dark, varying the route at times to avoid any particular one being too well known by outsiders. So skilled were these 'runners' that they could pick up a cargo on the beach after dusk and be in the Hurtwood by sunrise. This might involve thirty miles or more of winding paths and trackless heathland, but all concerned knew that their efforts would be well rewarded. Before daylight the contraband would be well hidden – perhaps in hollows dug out of the soft sand, or concealed among the thorns and brambles at the top of Combe Bottom. On more than one occasion a hollow tomb in Cranleigh churchyard was used as a hiding place. Some of the villagers found out about this and lay in wait in the porch nearby one night. Sure enough, the smugglers arrived but the Cranleigh men's courage failed them and they allowed the dreaded Heathers to creep away unapprehended.

The Windmill Inn, near the Ewhurst windmill itself, was a favourite gathering place for the smugglers after a successful 'run'. There they might relax till night fell again when they reclaimed their hidden contraband to take it on to London or possibly more local markets. It was rare for the few underpaid, and overworked, Revenue men then to intervene, although 'Bloody Banks', the name given to the track leading up into the Huntwood from Hoe Farm, is said to have been the scene of a battle between smugglers and enforcement officers. The goods seem to have been concealed more from local people and other smugglers than from the few Revenue men. If a stranger did happen to come across a smugglers' cache of brandy-kegs, it was the recognised practice to mark one or two with a chalk cross. The marked kegs would then be left behind when the smugglers returned, to be collected later by the finder as the price for his silence.

When the heavy import duties were abolished in the last century, smuggling ceased to be profitable. The ill-feeling between the Heathers and the lowland villagers continued nevertheless. The first policeman appointed at Peaslake in the opening years of this century had the job of putting an end to the annual fight between the Peaslakers and the Gomshall boys. There was also a 'battle' arranged on every Whit Monday at the Boy and Donkey Inn in Knowle Lane outside Cranleigh. There are conflicting accounts as to the combatants: certainly the youths of Cranleigh fought as one side, against the young men of Ewhurst, or Coneyhurst Hill, or Pitch Hill. It would seem from this that, to Cranleigh folk at least, the Ewhursters counted as Heathers. No description of this annual 'battle' survives, and it seems to have been discontinued before 1870. (The local tradition is that the battle commemorates a skirmish during the Civil Wars, when a body of cavalry was ambushed and defeated in Horseblock Hollow. As is often the case, local tradition is wrong. There was no such skirmish and the story was probably suggested by the place-name.) The nick-names given to either side in the Whit Monday battle are still not completely forgotten, though. Ewhursters are still known as 'Roundheads' to some, and Cranleigh men as 'Diamond Tops'. Whether or not these refer to the supposed shape of their respective heads is unclear, but these local jibes may be the last vestiges of the antagonism which existed before the Hurtwood became the civilised and respectable place it is today.

Retribution
by
Rough Music

IN THE CLOSE-KNIT village communities of old Surrey, everybody's business was, in effect, everyone else's. There was little that did not soon become general knowledge through gossip and rumour. In some cases this could be beneficial. For example, an old widow who fell and broke her hip would not be left lying on her cottage floor for long. Her failure to make some expected appearance would be noticed and some benevolent, or inquisitive, neighbour would investigate. On the other hand, it was hard to keep a secret – and if the secret was a shameful one, it might be punished. There were many ways of offending the moral attitudes of the community which were not actually against the law. In these cases the villagers would take the law into their own hands: the culprit might be ostracised or boycotted – or in severe cases given the Rough Music.

A graphic account of Rough Music refers to the Woking district in the middle of the last century. 'When a person has insulted the parish, by, say, beating his wife, or has committed some crime for which the law cannot punish him, the commoners and others collect old pans and pails,

and anything else that will make a hideous row and visit
the offender some evening unexpectedly. They surround
the house, banging their implements and yelling; at such
times people with harsh voices are at a premium, and
those who can perform very badly are eagerly welcomed if
they can bring their instruments of torture with them. The
performance winds up by their calling the culprit oppro-
brious names and smashing his windows.' Other accounts
mention stones rattled in tins, cows' horns, kettles and tin

trays, and instances of this custom are to be found from all over Surrey. Usually it is the village youths who were involved, sometimes disguised so as to remain anonymous, though in the Woking case quoted above, the nucleus of the rough musickers was composed of the choir of a parish church outside the district. They were invited in by a secret gathering of villagers in the pub who actually passed the hat round for their expenses. Perhaps it was thought that outsiders could more easily escape any repercussions or perhaps this choir was particularly noted for its awful voices. In any event it would be a thick-skinned individual who continued in his unacceptable ways after such a midnight serenade of communal disapproval.

By far the commonest crime which merited Rough Music was wife-beating, which seems by all accounts to have been almost a national sport. A particular refinement of Rough Music for wife-beating was noted by Gertrude Jekyll, when a girl in Bramley in the 1850s. A warning was given to the offender by laying a train of chaff up the path to the cottage door. Seeing it next morning, the brutal husband would realise that the villagers knew that 'thrashing' was going on in his house. If he then failed to mend his ways, he would be sure to wake one night to the discordant strains of the Rough Music.

The practice was not a purely rural one. The town saw its rough musicians as well. In Guildford in 1890, a chemist who beat his wife threw her out into the street. A mob of town youths and passers-by gathered and gave him the Rough Music, smashing the large carboys of coloured water in his window. Constable Drake of the Guildford Borough Police watched this rumpus for some while before moving in – to arrest the chemist. The authorities often turned a blind eye to these activities if they thought the victim deserved his fate.

However, wife beating was not the only crime so punished and in many cases the police dispersed a mob which

87

was kicking up a row over a wide variety of offences. An old man who married a young woman could expect an uproar outside his house, as at Richmond in 1874 and indeed Rough Music seems to have been a common feature of weddings generally. In Kew in 1874 the crowd serenading a shoemaker on his wedding day demanded drinks from him before they would go away. An adulteress at Peaslake in the early years of this century was rough musicked and thrown in the village pond and in 1889 the Rector of Abinger received rough treatment at the hands of some forty of his parishioners who disapproved of his levelling some graves in the churchyard. In the hard and hungry year of 1816 a crowd of some four hundred rough musicked a baker on Guildford High Street who had raised his prices, until the Mayor had to read the Riot Act. And a hungry gang of underpaid hop-pickers similarly voiced their disapproval of their employer in Farnham in the 1860s, carrying a penny loaf and a red herring on a hop-pole as a standard.

Thus Rough Music can be seen as a means whereby the ordinary people could protest about what they saw as threats to the stability of their community, and which the authorities were unable or unwilling to correct. Nowadays there are usually official ways of righting these grievances, and incidents of Rough Music in Surrey are rare after 1914 – though it was practised in Elstead during the Second World War, when it was known as 'Drumming Out'. Still, there are numerous things that go on today which offend popular opinion and morality, and it may be that Surrey nights will again be made horrible with the din of Rough Music.

Turnpikes
and the
King's Highway

T HE CHALK AND CLAY of Surrey do not make for good
roads, and overland journeys in the past were often
hampered by sticky mud in winter and choking dust in
summer. The Wealden iron industry had a damaging
effect on the roads in the south of the county, as carts
laden with fuel, ore, and iron cut into their surfaces.
Elizabethan regulations ordered that ironmasters must
repair the roads they used with cinder, slag or stone. Like
many Tudor laws, however, this one seems largely to have
been ignored. The main roads were not only poorly-surfaced
but often their direction across the heathlands of Surrey
could scarcely be distinguished. Strangers would hire a
local man to guide them on the correct route. The side
roads were, if possible, worse, and many of the lanes
through the sandy part of the county are deeply sunken,
evidence of centuries of traffic having eroded their soft
surfaces. Little was done that was effective in improving
Surrey's road until the coming of the turnpikes.

The turnpikes were a way of 'privatising' the King's
Highway. The re-surfacing and maintenance of certain
stretches of road became the responsibility of trusts, which
had the right to collect tolls at gates along the route. The

gates were originally horizontal bars pivoting on a central post – the 'turnpikes' after which the roads were named. The money collected went, in part, to repair the roadway, but the proportion paid as a dividend to the trustees was inevitably high. Turnpikes were introduced in Charles II's time; the first in Surrey was not opened, however, until 1696. This was a causeway across the Weald clay from Reigate to Crawley, but surprisingly it had a row of wooden posts down the centre to prevent wheeled traffic using it. It was thought, quite correctly, that horses' hooves would cause less damage to the new highway than carts or waggons. This curious arrangement lasted until 1755, when the Sutton to Reigate turnpike was completed. The road from London to Sutton had already been turnpiked in 1718, so now it was possible for wheeled traffic to run on decent roads from London to Brighton.

The Portsmouth road had a similar history of becoming turnpiked piecemeal over many years. The London to Kingston road had been improved in 1718 and in 1724 another turnpike was set up from Kingston to Burnt Common, near Ripley. This was extended in 1749 through Guildford to Petersfield, which had been linked by turnpike to Portsmouth since 1711.

In this way the two great Surrey highways, the Brighton road and the Portsmouth road, became established. Other routes followed: from London via Egham to Bagshot in 1727, then on to Farnham in 1753 on the Southampton road. Epsom, Leatherhead, Dorking, and Horsham were linked in 1755, after the people of Horsham had complained to Parliament that to reach London they had to travel by way of Canterbury! The Guildford to Arundel turnpike opened in 1757, and the following year saw others from Guildford to Leatherhead and Farnham. Finally, in 1764, the Petworth road from Milford was turnpiked, giving the county a network of main roads which saw little change until the motor-car stimulated road construction in the present century.

With a few exceptions, the turnpikes followed the routes of roads that had existed since the Middle Ages or earlier. However, the advantages of the improved road surfaces soon became obvious. Before 1749, for example, the seventy-mile journey from London to Portsmouth had taken 14 hours. It was the usual practice, in fact, to allow two days, spending the night in one of the half-dozen great coaching inns of Guildford. When the turnpike opened, however, this time was cut to as little as 9 hours, by coaches changing horses at 10 to 12 mile stages.

The Brighton road developed several alternative routes, the principal ones running through Croydon or Reigate. Both met at Povey Cross, near Gatwick, and ran south across what is now the airport runway to the Sussex border at the County Oak. Some Brighton traffic also went by way of Leatherhead and Dorking, or Caterham and Godstone to East Grinstead. A new turnpike in 1807 from Croydon avoided the steep hill into Reigate and the tunnel dug beneath Reigate Castle in 1823 saved sixty yards of the journey!

The Royal Mail, formerly carried on horseback, began to travel by coach to Portsmouth in 1784 and Brighton in 1791. This heralded the heyday of the turnpikes in the years following the end of the Napoleonic Wars. Crack coaches like the 'Red Rover' and the 'Rocket' endeavoured to break the record for their routes, and dozens of stage-coaches and private carriages passed up and down the main routes each day.

In November 1832 a portent appeared on the Brighton road: Walter Hancock's steam-powered coach 'The Infant'. In the event, the steam coach was slower than the stage-coach – but it was the steam locomotive that was to eclipse both. The coming of the railways saw the end of the coaching era and on the Portsmouth turnpike, for example, receipts dropped by a third. When the Royal Mail began to be sent to Portsmouth by train in 1842 it signalled the decline of the turnpikes. Less and less long-distance traffic went through the toll-gates and from 1862 onwards local Highway Boards began to take over from the unprofitable trusts. The gates on the Portsmouth road were taken off their hinges when the trust was wound up in 1870, but the Brighton turnpike lingered until 1881, the last in Surrey to become a free road.

Little now survives to remind us of this episode in our history. Many of the toll-houses have been demolished for road widening, though on the green verges of Surrey's main roads there still can be seen many of the old milestones – standing almost like the gravestones of the once flourishing turnpikes.

Headless Horsemen
and other
Horrors

Belief in ghosts is probably as widespread today as it ever has been in the past. Many would consider the very idea of ghosts to be an empty superstition, but I have spoken to too many sober and intelligent people who believe that they have seen ghosts to dismiss them so lightly. On the other hand, I have never seen one myself and so I lack the direct experience necessary to state with confidence that there are such things. Perhaps my viewpoint is best summed up by the old countryman who, when asked if he believed in ghosts, replied 'Oh no, but I'm mortal afraid of 'em'.

Human figures are by far the most frequently reported apparitions – indeed it seems a wonder that anyone can walk half a mile in Surrey without bumping into some 'grey lady' or other. There are, though, a significant number of tales that refer to phantom coaches. Two notable examples come from opposite sides of the county: Chelsham and Farnham

Slines Pond lies a the junction of Slines Oak Road and the Limpsfield Road near Warlingham. Here, they say, a coach once came to grief, driving deep into the pond and drowning its occupants. It is seen again, so the story goes, rising up out of the pond 'all lit up, with passengers screaming at the windows'. Details vary in different tellings of the tale. Some say it was a highwayman that frightened the horses, others that a thunderstorm caused them to bolt. One elaborate account claims that this accident took place in November 1809 because the driver was drunk. It was a Royal Mail coach and both the passengers and the horses were drowned. It is almost needless to add that there is no record of any such accident taking place at that date. Nevertheless, the story is widespread in the area and a coach that appears at Riddlesdown nearby is reputed to be one that met with a fatal accident – perhaps linked in imagination, if nothing else, with the Slines Pond 'disaster'.

The Hop Bag in Downing Street, Farnham, is said to see the re-enactment of a tragic episode of Georgian times. A young girl was waiting in the yard for her sweetheart, who was due to arrive on the London coach. It did not come at the appointed time, unusual and disturbing in an age when timekeeping was very strict on the coaching routes, and as the minutes passed the poor girl began to worry. Alas, her fears were all too well founded. When the coach finally clattered up, her lover was not on board. His lifeless body lay on the road far behind, shot by a highwayman who had held them up. The Hop Bag, it is said, is still haunted by the rumble and rattle of the iron-shod wheels and hooves of the coach and horses whose lateness aroused anxiety but whose arrival brought despair.

It is a curious phenomenon in this tale that only the sound of the coach is heard, without any visible manifestation. This is also the case in reports from Limpsfield, Abinger, and Great Bookham. On the other hand, when the Rector of Ash saw a phantom coach drive through the Rectory in 1938 he saw it very clearly indeed: 'I was awakened by the thud of horses hooves and the sound of a horn. The coach came in the back way and drove straight through the house and made towards the church. I saw the coachman distinctly. He was wearing a scarlet seventeenth or eighteenth century uniform. He seemed quite a cheerful person, and I am distinctly under the impression that he turned round as I gazed after him and gave me a

cheery salutation with his whip. I have not seen this phantom coach since, but I do not mind if I do. If the rectory must have a ghost, it is as well that it should be a jolly one.'

Some stories tell of headless coachmen – one from Horsell, indeed, tells of a coach whose horses were likewise headless. This would surely have made them very difficult to control unless, as the horsemen say, the driver gave them their head. The road south of Godstone was reputed in the last century to be haunted by a headless driver of a coach and four, which appeared at midnight, rattling and creaking on its eternal journey. One night in about 1882 a young woman who lived at Quarry Cottage was walking home from Blindley Heath alone. The night was dark and eerie and the girl's imagination soon turned to ghosts – to the ghostly coach of which she had been told. She heard the clock strike midnight when she was only a hundred yards from her cottage – but then heard the hoofbeats and rattling of a fast-driven coach coming up behind her. She ran frantically to her garden gate and pulled at it. It refused to open, and as she tugged and tugged in mounting terror the sound drew closer and closer. As the coach came clattering up to her, the maiden fell to the ground insensible. The coachman, who was provided with a perfectly ordinary head, had been driving some guests home after a party at Marden. He drew up his horses and jumped down when he saw the unconscious girl, and helped her to recover her senses and calm her fears. He also helped her through her own front gate – by pushing it open.

Many of our fears, I am sure, are similarly of our own making and as long as people need some sort of mystery in their lives, then phantom coaches will continue to travel the roads of Surrey.